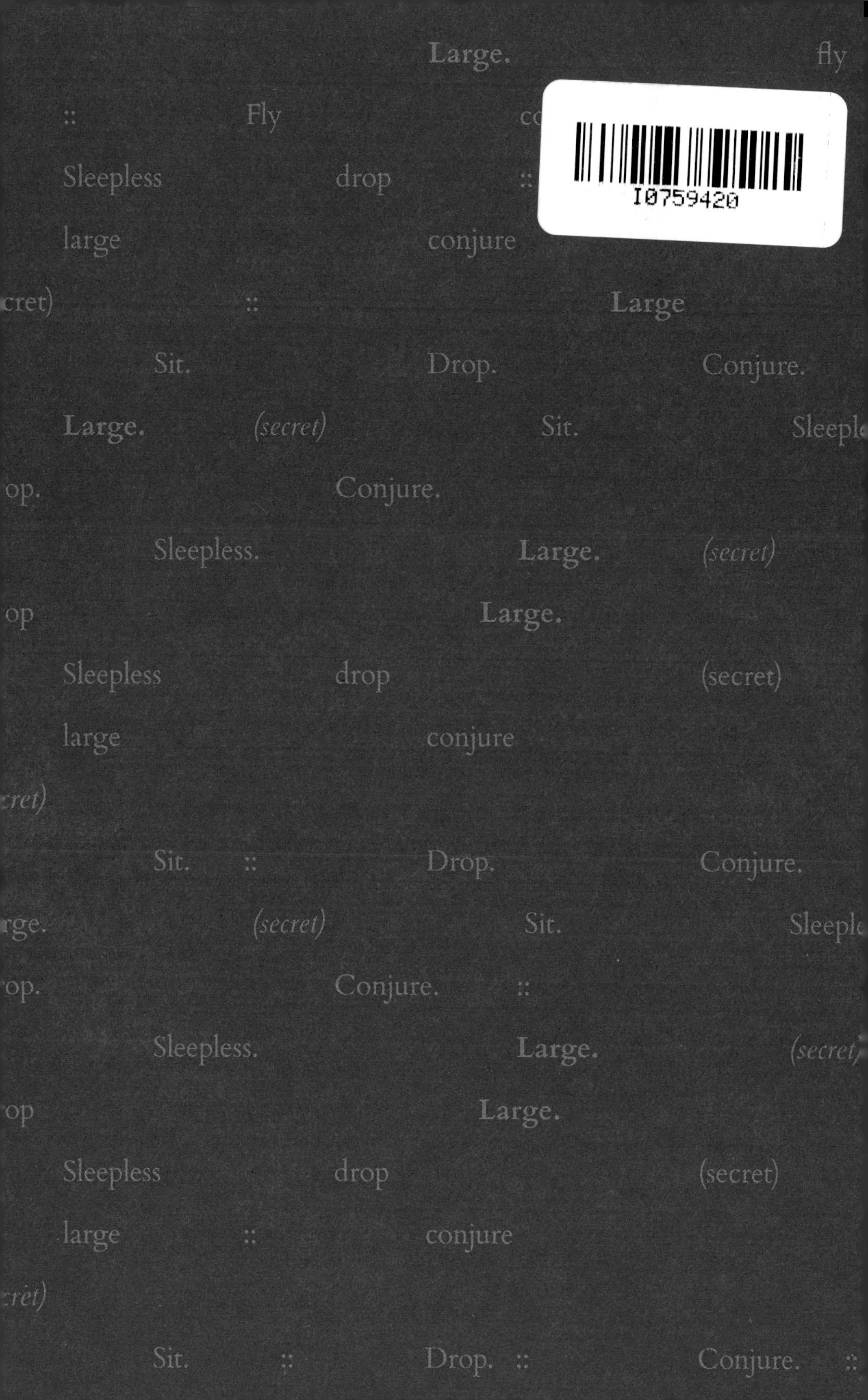
Large. fly
:: Fly co
Sleepless drop ::
large conjure
cret) :: Large
Sit. Drop. Conjure.
Large. (secret) Sit. Sleepl
op. Conjure.
Sleepless. Large. (secret)
op Large.
Sleepless drop (secret)
large conjure
cret)
Sit. :: Drop. Conjure.
rge. (secret) Sit. Sleepl
op. Conjure. ::
Sleepless. Large. (secret)
op Large.
Sleepless drop (secret)
large :: conjure
cret)
Sit. :: Drop. :: Conjure. ::
I0759420

MORE BOOKS BY SAMIYA BASHIR

POETRY COLLECTIONS

Field Theories

Gospel: poems

Where the Apple Falls: poems

LIMITED EDITION ARTISTS' BOOKS

M A P S :: a cartography in progress
(with Yornel J. Martínez Elías & Tracy Schlapp)

Hades D.W.P.
(with Alison Saar & Tracy Schlapp)

EDITED VOLUMES

Best Black Women's Erotica 2

Role Call: A Generational Anthology of Social & Political Black Literature & Art
(with Tony Medina & Quraysh Ali Lansana)

POETRY CHAPBOOKS

Teasing Crow & Other Haiku

American Visa

Wearing Shorts on the First Day of Spring

PRAISE FOR *I HOPE THIS HELPS*

I Hope This Helps presents readers with a kind of Samiya-Bashirian Ode, teeming with lucid music, candid witness, and radical play. These poems blend levity and gravity, joy and sadness; they meld genres of memoir, essay, and art. The Bashirian Ode is a testament of inner and outer empathy: the ways we study and care for ourselves and others. *I Hope This Helps* is akin to an illustrated, illuminated guidebook, a lantern of language for surviving dark times.

—TERRANCE HAYES

I Hope This Helps—a title I wish I thought of—is a formal field day of genre-bending innovation from cross-outs to blackouts to music scores, all held together by a voice so singular it may well remind you of your own. If Samiya Bashir is apologetic in these poems, she means to apologize to herself. If she is encouraging—and thank God she is—it is to bring her own self back to the task: "The work must become if it is ever to matter—like life." This book is Bashir's magnum opus. I'm so glad I got to read it.

—JERICHO BROWN

Samiya Bashir's *I Hope This Helps* is exuberant, choreographed cartography, improvisational typography, each page carrying the prints of a real human being/s, collaborative, lost-and-found, ekphrasis until it must bleed into real linotype (sometimes words just don't carry the tune), sheet music, blank page of kindergarten paper and I feel the shame, monstrous performance, performance of Monster, self-address, us-addressed, no-address, home-as-road-becomes-the-road-home, history and tyranny, both literary and not, Eliot's "The Waste land" to Asghar's "Pluto Shits on the Universe," June Jordan to Amiri Baraka, Reagan to Trump, plague to plague, bulletproof vest to bulletproof poem, killer bees to killer knees, quoting June Jordan quoting Auschwitz survivor Elly Gross, "And what shall we do," she asked, "we who did not die? What shall we do now? How shall we grieve, and cry out loud, and face down despair?" Quoting Maxine Hong Kingston, "In a time of destruction, create something." I read Samiya Bashir and it registers—something has been created. Something has been created titled *I Hope This Helps*. This reader's answer: It does.

—DIANE SEUSS

A genre bending beacon and everything we need right now.

—JACQUELINE WOODSON

Of what practical value is a life in art? What knowledge do we produce that provides the means to sustain light and understanding to life? Samiya Bashir's *I Hope This Helps*. starts with some of the right questions in our screw-tightening times with admirable candor, curiosity, and generative tangent. What do we do to live and thrive—as Black people, joyous and queer, new neighbors and strangers, our full humanity—dwarfed in the shadows by towers of power, distraction, and fear? Bashir's poetry leans into these questions using her superpower—pausing to listen—over-hearing and hearing over—"hearing" under and re-writing, reinscribing her journey—through the "twinkle-textured disco-ball Jenga set"—and shows the reader how creative power fuels us to begin again. And again.

—ERICA HUNT

I Hope This Helps is a map that shapeshifts with each reading. Beheld, it holds, beholds the "meaning of a moment like ours."

—JEN BERVIN

I HOPE THIS HELPS

I HOPE THIS HELPS

SAMIYA BASHIR

NIGHTBOAT BOOKS
NEW YORK

Printed in the United States

ISBN: 978-1-64362-272-9

Design and typesetting by Kit Schluter
Typeset in **AM TRIPOLI** & Cardo

Cataloging-in-publication data is available
from the Library of Congress

Nightboat Books
New York
www.nightboat.org

for Fofie

—

la mia costante

"I want to thank me for believing in me."

NIECY NASH

CONTENTS

THE DRESSMAKER
THE ACCOUNTANT
THE HANDMAID
THE INTERPRETER
THE OTHER SISTER
THE OTHER WOMAN
THE TOURIST

. . .

THE HELP

listen:

we ain't all well

this world
spins designs
which madden
us shape us
like dough
bake us crisp

there may be those
who will crumble us
into paving for their own roads

listen: we mustn't let them but

also—

          love—

we aren't all well

we can't all resist
as well as we might

we can't all fight
enough or at all and

I can’t say how we heal

I wish
I could

I would

I’ll try:

ACHERON

what use

this inoculation

inch after

useless inch

dip
dip
dip

come back

please?

what use-
less pleas

how much longer?

how much?

A LAND

SCAPE

■ ■ ■

OBVIOUSLY

Sit :: Sleepless :: Drop :: Conjure :: Fly. :: **Large.** **Large.** *(secret)* Yes. Question yourself. Question all those who meet you. Doubt. You were given birth to by notions formulated in heads. You were not a child. Breathing just like anybody else. Exist. Think. Yes that's the word. That is not the heavens. Unless there are. Unless.

When your uncle speaks. On your behalf. Wonder. Of friends. *(creatures of fiction)* Whose likes and **dislikes**. Are a blood relation. Leap to the tongue. Prodigious imagination. Ceased to exist as beings. Journeys to a region. Solid and prominent. The way blind people's eyes tend to. Numb of soul. You are not yourself. Anyway. Numerous doorways. Are enabled. Through forests. Without any clearing. Stone steps too numerous to count. In the wake of the old man. There was a girl. A butcher. Knowing what knives of destiny await.

I

HOPE

THIS

HELP

OVERHEARD

The trouble with arrival is how it feels
so finite:

Journey toward destination,
then arrive,
then the end.

Journey complete.

My own experience is of beginning again. And again. And again. Not from scratch each time, which is the real gift, but more like a builder, more like a twinkle-textured disco-ball Jenga set, journey and arrival spin above my head—where every bit and shard can come crumbling down at any time—and does so
each time I pull a foundational piece of
structure.

But—sometimes—that itch—that tight skin—must—pull!

•

I'm the eldest child of an eldest child. I spent most of my little years surrounded by grown-ups who talked about grown-up things and lived their grown-up lives all while I—silent and usually unseen—watched, listened. Strong sense memory stories include an embrace of quiet invisibility and its helpmate: piping up to go along for the ride. I'd slip across a back seat and disappear into overhearing.

To grow up was to know all the ways to catch snatches of things that I wasn't supposed to know yet.

Thing is:
structures aren't forever,
needn't be—for me, at least—shouldn't be.

To wit:
I left the Bay Area for NYC in the 1990s because I needed the kind of pressure that can shatter as well as shape. Whether true or not, at that time I felt that I could quite literally anti-grow as an artist and remain comfortable as a person. As an artist, celebrated, even brave—or some shit—no one, then and there, seemed to ask me that coal-crushing, facet-forcing Jacksonian query:

What have you done for me lately?

So then—
to shape or to shatter
perhaps a question more of *when* and *where*
than of *if*. Sometimes, one must shatter. Often
there is often no other way
to grow.

Making a life, for me, has always been a quest for time—through time—a wrestling with competing needs for both structure and time unrestricted. They seem opposites, but my consistent work is to figure out how to get them to live in concert.

To wit:
Bill Bixby didn't become Lou Ferrigno
without ripping through
shredding his every piece
of clothing.
Never
not one time
was his Jekyll-fit

undisturbed. Safe.
    Same. Never,
        not once.

Now, a thing that can drive a body to distraction is pain.

And, fact of the matter is, shattering hurts.

But, quiet as it isn't even kept, so does shaping and sculpting and form.

So does stillness and its often-coincident rot—I think of the bound foot, of the clipped bonsai,
    orthopedics and orthotics,
        levees which contain/constrain their rivers,
            shapewear which constricts breath and matter
                not to break
                    but to construct.

"IT'S ALL SO PERFORMATIVE." That overheard sentence, which inserted itself into my thinking and writing with some kind of truth, is also true.

I'm not, like, anti-stillness—I just don't know her. But that's another essay I'll likely never write. Let's be real, I would be nowhere without it: stillness, its silence, its noise, its performance. And yet, here I am, tasked to consider whether and why any of it—my work, its maker—even matters.

Thing is—I overhear but from the inside—I gotta make new recent work.

(Deep Breath.)

•

So, according to the literature, I'm a disordered eater. Food is both delicious and a horrendously arduous undertaking.

And it's like that, this whole writing thing. I can't exactly not do it if I hope to maintain even a moderate facsimile of sanity. Likewise, to maintain even a moderate facsimile of health—even, life—I gotta eat. No matter what the Soylent boys say. No matter what I'd rather do. I don't usually eat very well. But still, I've gotta.

I don't usually write very well either. But the Muse Industrial Complex makes certain guarantees. The more I write, the more some things make sense—even if only to me; and if I'm honest, most of the world seems completely senseless, even if only to me.

The thing about having no choice is that one does have a choice about whether or not to share what one leaks from one's being. Just because a thing needs writing doesn't mean it needs reading. Most things I write don't need sharing. That understanding—oh dear—I fear is like acting. One makes or writes or performs because one must. One shares because this time, this piece, this moment, might actually matter, to someone, someone else—that's the thing—someone, even, who you can't yet imagine.

Even now, I look back on pieces I've written which I find literally cringe-inducing—but *that's*—as my inner ego+id couple's counselor might say—*my* shit. Often I learn that whatever I want to burn is something so meaningful to someone else that I'm blown, like match flame, back to humility. Once returned, I'm reminded how much this whole business of writing, of sharing, is just not about me, and for good reason.

If I still stanned (in eons-old-already parlance) something I wrote thirty years ago in San Francisco, then I wouldn't be growing as an artist. Uncomfortable as it may be, my own artistic ontogenesis remains as essential as shedding old skin to stretch into the new.

Birthing? Cleaving? Extricating? Whatever.

All nerve endings, I overhear, and beauty.

As artists we are trained to lean into reverence for the ego at what seems to be every turn. But the work (Occam's razor?) leverages our labor to bring it into existence and then gallops off—or in—once made, on its own terms to live its own life (n)either with us (n)or despite us.

What matters to this writer then is *that* the work matters rather than why the work matters. Like my Black-ass life, one lets *why* get in the way; suddenly one is working to imagine or create the *why* rather than the *what*, rather than the thing itself. The work must *become* if it is ever to matter—like life.

AND WHAT AM I TO BE—RAW OUT HERE? Entrails all exposed? Skinless?! Nah, B! Nawwwww.

•

For most of my life I was the young kid in the crowd, friends and family near-universally older than me. Before we were so obsessed by generational actuarial tables, I was the perfect age to watch too many mentors die too young of AIDS and cancer and general neglect. Yes, that part. But also, there's me:

I'm a bit exoskeleton-y—lone-wolf-y—
          a bit lioness-y, yet
                    a bit hide-y from my pride-y. Yet and

still, I learned to listen early enough to become an Olympic-level amateur overhearer. Still and yet through various mentorships—some of us, always June Jordan reminds, do/did not (yet) die—I learned the ways and hows which attend the work of listening.

For instance: Just get in the car. Pipe up to go along for the ride. I've learned more on many a store run than I have in entire terms of class time.

The people you admire? Those from whom you can learn? Be of service.

What I know is that I've gained more from fetching someone a drink or a tissue than from many a structured interview. We are all, in all ways, our asides.

These are among those ways to be with—to be in place to grow, to ether-learn, to overhear.

•

By this part of the page the night is long-legged and middle-aged, like me, so I'll share a secret: Everything takes me a thousand times longer to do / to make / to become than it might seem. No matter the length of my stride.

No matter how many machines I manipulate. No matter what plethora of apps and screens, I keep finding in myself the need to pare down, to slow. Most of my writing gets done by hand—I'm trying to say—despite the wild digitalia of our world. Imagine. In this, the year of our capitalist clock 2,000-plus, it's strange to say, but stranger to realize, considering I don't do much journaling.

That's a lie, but only kind of. What it is, really, is a shame.
My life is kind of fascinating. ¯_(ツ)_/¯

But something about trust is missing there
where intention lives / lays / lies.

•

My mother has always, at least as long as I've known her, had the television on, the radio, the record player.

My sisters and me? It's the podcasts. The millennials among us can even make whole televisions out of phones sans annoyance or loudly acknowledged needs for emergency chiropracty.

So, I understand my mother's desire for sound, digital company, the comfort of conversation, even if it's only one-sided. Even now, I write by hand, outside, surrounded by strangers in conversation. I may as well be in the world's back seat. Still too small to see over the front bucket seats, I peer through the middle by ear. And it's the best of both and all. No one is talking to me. I can listen or not. I needn't pay attention. But I'm also not left alone to my silence. Still.

And yet, I need it—that silence, its poetry. But
sometimes I also need it to leave me 'lone.

"That's the way," I interrupt the overheard speaker, "to do prison, I figure."
"I got lot of fuckin' writing done," she replied. Fait accompli.

•

What does it mean to write with the never-silence of breath?

To write with space
with absence and color—

if I read a poem, how is it read
by my color-blind friend?

Does their sight
newly right my stanzas?
Rewrite my melodics?

Does my red sound brown?

Will it gray?

I have a friend who is, in fact, a great painter, a major artist, even. I like to wear the coats she no longer wears—her hand-me-overs. They always have paint on them somewhere. Not great art or anything, just drips and smears, leavings and stains.

And me? On occasion I can't help but write a poem. But on more important occasions I am able to sculpt poetry from the raw material of writing, reading, listening.

That's the *can't stop*. That's the must do. It's not as if I can't stop creating beauty or writing poetry or making work—it's actually remarkably rare that I do any of those things. But writing? It's a constant, like a tic, a twitch, a security blanket. It's like a dictionary for the only language I'm allowed to speak but am also, always, (s)training to learn.

ATT
EN
TI
ON

OUR PAIN

OUTLASTS

she taught you | how best | you should make use | of
your own body | she assisted you
like the day's shadow | from the | purposelessness | of
our own body | your soul | your brain | she couldn't
hurt herself

    not then | anyway
    was this why she went | ?

she nourished you | a body | totally her own | young as
you were | needy and self-sufficient | she could choose
to be herself | walk | about | in the nude | if she
wanted | when awake | if you were the only person in
the room | she cursed people | in her language | it
didn't matter whether you understood | or not | what
mattered | was the look in your eyes
                                        surprise
or incomprehension | yours and | hers | because of her
relations with you | you | became a controversial topic
| to many | she was
                                        from
    somewhere else
    , up north"

they treated her | despicably | calling her | all sorts of
things | no one took the trouble | to reach the bottom |

who was she really?

to you, she was the cosmos | hers was the body | upon which your growing | nourished | it didn't matter | in the least | whether she came | or not | if she had been a warrior | or no | she meant the world to you

NO ONE ELSE NEEDED HER

AS MUCH AS YOU

as often as you | when she wasn't | with you | with a self-abandon | you cried and cried | with a self- | surrender | some say | she bewitched you things fall apart.

I am sort of sleeping then
I am on fire. Undone. Burned.
Stripped of skin I feel so
raw these days. Flattened.
Full of doubt. Numb.

Rats thrive in sewers so
maybe I'm thriving. It may seem
simple enough but my dreams don't
say so. This I think I know: no one
notices me. Lost. Alone. Blind
as a sewer rat. Six feet back. Gelatinous.
Raw as a baby rat. Shook. Underdone.
Too-full rat still hungry. Rich rat swimming
sewage. Breadline rat. Baker rat. Transformed. Stuck
in a well. Thriving. Burned into brick
road. Milepost. Sign.

Triumphant. I scream but
words burn like skyfire. Clammy.
Street rat. Fell in a hole. Stuck
in a well. I rattle the cages of our
children. Everywhere else
is empty.

I am not saying I'm a prophet but
I know the meaning of a moment

like ours. Burning. I'm almost sure
I'm here. Transformed. Torn apart.
Average. Boring. Humdrum. Numb.
No sound stays innocent. I am

fluent in fire. Fluent in indigo
miseries. I am fluent in the absence of
heat. A rat on the street. Sudden and melt.
I am fluent in how time presses
a body. Here's the thing I'm not
supposed to say: I saw others skulk
the dark like me. Simple enough.
I skulk away a little more each day.
Maybe there's intelligent life
but I'm not it. How will we survive this
having a body? Trying to be
intelligent life. Fireball struck and stuck.
I study the crows who know this—having
a body to fly.

Almost a dream. A sign
you're not supposed to notice. A path.
Who can I be? Blame the apocalypse.
Its melt. Its bends. It never ends.

Thing is: things fall apart. Everyday

the end of the world is now again. Normal.
I burn and remember having a body. How
it feels. Cold. If I hold no beauty in this slapdash
world, then tuck me away from the heat of the day.

Alone. I burn. Blame the humdrum
numbness of the end of the world. Listen for
the wind. Intelligent life: where is it? No sound
an innocent means. Route. Way. I am

not saying I'm a prophet but I always travel
slightly singed. Pressed by time. Six feet back
I find the me who's tall as a gum tree, the me
with copper hair. Causeway me. Opening.

Expanse.
Eyes open, heart full of doubt.
I strike my fireballs and burn. Sort of
dreaming. Now volcano. Now oil-slicked
river. Stripped of skin. Fluent
in the press of time. Body clammed. Voice
raw and syrup stripped. Eyes open. Sewer rat.
Thriving. No sound stays innocent.
Rats.

Footpath. Corridor. Clearing and
yes the bushes burn like skyfire. And
I decide to survive. Claim every sunrise.
I am dark as earth. Now I am me with the
bright yellow hair. Me with a normal
girth—wait—

Normal? Do I know that word? Did I ever? Is it
normal to hang from a tree? Is normal an ability
to breathe? Are normal these panic attacks?
Does normal stand whole bodies back? Tucked

away from the heat of the day, I listen for how to survive
this body. Face twisted. Slightly singed. Fueled
by my own crisped flames. Condemned.

I know the meaning of a moment but here's the thing:
Am I intelligent life? Pffft. How could I tell? The crows know.
I know I'm not road. I'm doorway. And when things fall apart
again I'll be here—my rectangular shade of blue. I'm not
supposed to talk about transformation though. Not the me
with the hollow cheeks. The me with the blood-red stride.
Fluent in the need to dance.

Me with moles in fourteen places. Here.
Having a body. Me with three nose rings. Normal.
I grasp for a branch. Normal. I thrive. Gutter rat. Me
with the war wounds. The burning quiet of stars. The
crows know. Who else
can I be?

ANOTHER THIN FILAMENT PYROMETRY

wild turkeys strut
the yard
limp in the face of fulfillment look delicious and
the wind gusts and gusts—me? i await the woodpecker i love—

of course i call him, *him*
and Woody because woody-ass words like
hegemony   but   so—
                                        listen

don't ask me what matters

know

            or don't know maybe just do it
            over there.
            i'm tired.
            time's been so

untethered i want to
hammock in the sun
i wanna leave the machines
            with you
over there   by you   here
have 'em i just sigh

if we're gonna swing and swing the trees let us
hammock
in our own damned peace   or

don't
i mean
you could don't
sigh

ssssssshhhhhhhhhh
no
really
sssssssssssshhhhhhhhh

YES

OF COURSE

YOU

ARE

ALSO

RACIST

. . .

WELCOME

from your first encounter you didn't like the way
(s)he out-stared you

you paid her all attention leaving you
more or less yourself

your eyes the look described as (wicked)
(satanic) did not appear at all
convinced

not quite a being

perhaps this explains why she exists
primarily
upon
the fortune
of different
kingdoms the
living and the
dead

disappointed (again)

LETHE

it's over

struggle

it burns

remember

drink

forget

how quickly you laugh

forget

the absurdity of living

by my apple

i promise

nothing

i promise

nothing

i promise

no—

HISTORY
AS
NIGHTMARE

CRIME
AS
PALIMPSEST

LITERACY
AS
ERASURE

MAPS IV :: A CARTOGRAPHY IN PROGRESS

Allah is the space and time of all Muslims—

Allah is the space and time of all Muslims—

Allah is the space and time of all Muslims—

Allah is the space and time of all—
Muslims—

Allah is—the space—and time—of all—Muslims—

— — — — — — —

, but not you—

(as usual) :: resist :::::

she had organized her life
around you

she awoke (not)
to say her prayers
(but) (not)

to attend to your needs

was she you?
even-legged
sure-footed

but then how could—

HOW

DID I

BECOME THE

ALTERNATIVE

(NOT YOU)

?

NAIL HARD

—as i was saying
your
(idea of) death ain't mine(s)

i('ll) sprout any how

(flourish!)

your rot   flesh don't make me   no
          (ting)   never mind

—s t r e t c h—

not too long

(just) long enough (just)
dark(ish)   grow(th)

hard as illusion(s)
and furthermore—

AM REAL...

I AM REAL...

I AM REAL...

I AM REAL...

I AM REAL...

the small world of darkness cast by your stars
you opened your you
touch yourself in order to be reassured

in bed the priest was in his foulest
of moods you are touchably there
without reassuring yourself

"What am I to do then?"
"Be accommodating"
"You are insane"
"And you are jealous"
"You are never alone"

so much so that (I see you) all the time you
smell of urine

I JUST GO INTO WHATEVER BATHROOM MATCHES MY OUTFIT

THAT'S HOW EASY MY

CIS IS

SOMETIMES I DON'T EVEN

NOTICE

PLANE AFTER PLANE AFTER PLANE BUZZES

should i even try to cope
or is that just complicit?

maybe why
i just stayed high the entire
time not because my sofa
buttered me

when my life
ridiculouses again
i'll love it
i say

i promise
i am

so prepared
for disappointment i

shut tight the space around me i
ignore each breath of passing air i

play private living room with
two hundred other humans

such banal miracles all
glued to little televisions

does the pilot know how
not alone we are

in the clouds
like nothing
?

THE ONLY POEM

which roger, the trainer
said i'd have back
    home and also oh and
    own—and—ly—and my
                        own
                            lonely
                                poem

like there's only one like to
be alone is the worst kind of lonely when—

back home—mine a poem i make flip
        and shine and stretch but like
                stay passive about it
                        verbly you know—
                            leave me some subjectivity
                                    wait—

can i at least come home to my own goddamned subjectivity?

wait—

off track it's the fact of the
        speedspeed that the folks who say they're
smarter than me concede i need but all i remember is one man's
still   but   and   so   still   but   and   so
        and yet
            um
oh right—

        so roger trains with his dick, right? but i don't
        mind it so much—
                a personality quirk :: it gets the job done
                , really and and and and and and and and and and and and
and and and and and and and and and and and and and and and and and
and and and and and and and and and and and and and and and and and
and and and and and and and and and shit

oh right—
        wait—

where the fuck are my ~~meds~~ ~~drugs~~ ~~friends~~ ~~lovers~~ ~~cats~~ ~~memories~~ anyway?!
anyway?
      whatever. i'm so lonely only—
                        (i forgot).

TOO OFTEN I REMEMBER THE FUTURE

COCYTUS

all you are is

unoriginal food

well
          come

hold your head up

-kick-

  -ball-

    -change-

 (or don't)

i'd say i haven't

got all day but

—i whisper—

                    i do
you too

DULL CARE

I'll swim for inoculation, as Achilles I'll
splash behemothic through pool after pool
swim their lengths then back then back I fear I feel
I fear I've sunk too deep deep
like neck-deep ya know? Like
too deep to stand. Not afloat somehow
but head above the waterline somehow. Under
it's over—over I struggle to remember worth
I wonder how quickly through death's door
one laughs at absurd earthly cares. I know

we like to think the dead remember us
hover even—support surely—but isn't that
just so much hubris? A speck of a planet—a wee
moment—an experience—sort of—considering
shouldn't we dead be busy living really living
the lives we're up here waiting on? Then again
maybe it's selfish to think we're forgotten. Maybe
it's selfish to worry about selfishness. Maybe I'm
so self-centered I say we but mean me. A problem, you
know? A cultural thing I can't solve for. I can only lie

down and crave a cuddle.
Any cuddle. Any cuddle.

SORRY I'M

SORRY SO SORRY

SO SO SORRY

OMG I'M SO SORRY

SORRY

SO SO

SORRY SORRY

I'M SORRY

SO SORRY

I'M

CLAIRVOYANCE

what use is this inoculation?

i try to breathe
          pressure — it bruises

i'm too bruised to move

not sunlight
you're brighter than that
like waves pushed up
from up under

i see it
(pushed up) pushed up
from up under

i can see — me
ripple and shake
like water

why can't we just marry
you and I ?

and let our bodies join without odor and cries

(we cannot) in body and spirit too and no

I can be yours only in (sin) only in (sin)
only in (sin) imagine

you and

burst into tears

and

burst into tears

and

burst into tears

and

burst

FRIDAY

BROKE

HER

SHE STOPPED BELIEVING

LETTER FROM EXILE

2020

Oh, Dear.

Thrown away. Caught mid-toss.
I tried to write about everything except my own experience.
Time has become so untethered. Can I even remember Tuesdays?
Everything remains unresolved.

•

I am still, in theory, one of two 2019–20 Rome Prize Fellows in Literature. The year marked the 125th anniversary of the American Academy in Rome: a rare two-poet year. Bold and brilliant Nicole Sealey holds the second prize.

We are, together, the Academy's first Black women Literature Fellows. Ever. Being a Negro First(TM) just feels so last century.

•

I'm almost certain the Academy tried not to kick us out.

Do I remember certainty?

First, they kicked some of us out of our rooms, some out of our studios, some out of both. Word was we'd be shuffled, only temporarily, to maximize social distancing. For our safety.

The days groundhogged and caught. Food was altered. Then adjusted. Then gone. Our lives were pieced apart and jumbled around with an almost-impressive opacity.

We weren't allowed to leave our new shuffle-spaces. We were asked not to see each other. We sung from our rooftops and leaned through our windows to see each other.

•

Conflicting messages raced toward obsolescence. Now stock groceries, at least three weeks' worth. Now leave your groceries. Leave your belongings. Leave your projects. Leave your work. Leave home. Just leave.

You ain't gotta go home but you cain't stay here is what I hear being said when I remember it. We'd stood a meter apart, for our safety, across the steps. Some of us, just away for a day or a few, were told remotely: *You can't come home.*

And it was our home: Rome. And where were we supposed to go? Nearly everyone from New York had sublet their places. Someone else had just sold their house. I'd ended my lease months before landing in Rome. Everything was stored somewhere. Including me. In Rome. Until—

I was given two days—okay, less—to un-home myself. Borders were closing, they said, for our protection. Pack a life. Leave a life behind. Thrown away, one or two of us stayed despite it all. Ghosted the empty city streets in search of shelter. Home.

•

For decades I'd joked that home was somewhere around 33,000 feet. No more.

•

Do I remember planes?

Around dawn on the first day of spring we were flung, stiff-legged and bleary, from frying pan to fire. For our protection. The last Fellows in flight. The ways we clutched our rationed masks and overused gloves were, honestly, kinda sketch.

Leonardo da Vinci–Fiumicino Airport's once-bright gateways lay empty as old-timey Christmas Day. No Prada. No Gucci. No Valentino. Dark windows twinkled their shiny things. Everyone tried to avoid eye contact.

Onboard we shuffled to separate corners, then again for more social distancing. A flight attendant's ersatz alarm woke me when my mask slipped in my sleep.

•

Then magic and sisterhood and poetry and love and dreaming and trust all got together and gifted me a place to land by the sea. In one day. By nightfall. Imagine.

Take that, hope.

•

The first thing I saw as we landed ashore was a big-box store. Home. At JFK someone tested my temperature on the jet bridge. I guess I passed. Then the constant assault of commercials.

So many Cuomos.
So many talking heads loudly declaring war.
For my protection.

That our isolations showed neither violence nor oppression but care seemed so basic when I left Rome that it remained unspoken. Now "shelter-in-place" was a canyon echo. A Wile E. Coyote.

That language: it mattered.

"I guess a silver lining of all this," I've heard so often that I lost count, "is we get a break from school shootings."

•

The Venetian etymology of *ciao* is one of enslavement. Whether coming or going one said *schiavo*: I am your slave. This was, I guess, in case someone forgot.

So much about home is buried beneath every breath.

I remain your slave. Venice flooded but—dammit—

I wasn't there.

•

A very fine person met me outside of Logan Airport to take me home. We followed highway 3 to highway 6 talking (mostly him) through politics, through life.

He'd spent years building his livery business, he said. By March he'd already had to let every one of his drivers go. Now he, himself, was back to driving.

He noticeably avoided praising or defending our American president. No one wanted to fight that night. It was so late. We were so tired.

I couldn't say whether it had been moments or millennia since that last masked goodbye outside of customs in Brooklyn. Holding each other up. Taking pictures. Now the house on the hill sat cloaked in new-moon darkness. Like me. Alone.

•

To matter. To be important. To signify.

So well-curated we were an accident, my Romies & I. *I miei ragazzi.* Our hodgepodge had lived together, traveled, studied, worked, and eaten together every single day. Six months by then. Longer than COVID by then.

At first all I could do was mourn us and all we'd left shattered atop Gianicolo. That our hill was named for Janus—two-faced god of beginnings and endings, doorways and gates, transitions and time—felt ominous after having felt just right.

Exile. Loss. My heart sinks and sinks. At least two of us contracted Corona (*lungo anche*) on those flights back home. I spoke broken Italian for weeks, catching myself—*un po' di più*—each day.

•

Sembro la merda di un lupo quando parlo Italiano.

•

The year threads its needle between robbery and gift; horror and beauty. Global trauma and lovely surprises.

To wake up in Cape Cod! Shingles! Whippoorwill winds! A new old-fangled tide clock!

Quarantines require preparation. What did I know from hunkering? Shopping and setup and space and supplies met most of us who went home, but I wasn't met. I wasn't home.

The refrigerator was so empty it shone. My phone was hooked up to all the wrong satellites. All day I went out of my way not to touch anything. I covered my face and crept the Cape gathering whatever I guessed I might need.

Yes, toilet paper. Yes, tequila. Yes, flash-frozen soups and every kind of chip I could find.

I bathed in hand sanitizer at every stop. I tried to not be a stranger. I snapped through pair after pair of the latex gloves I'd used in my studio to dip ink just a whisper ago. I remembered that I'd left my ink atop Gianicolo.

That was the first day. There was another. And another.

It was good that I didn't have to do anything because I could barely breathe. I made my quarantine phone calls. I attributed my breath, my tight chest, to everything except my own experience.

•

I was almost sure my life mattered.

•

The thing about twenty-first-century Negro Firsting(TM) is that racism—the distraction of it as Morrison warned—is just so *boring*.

Yet another exhausting lack of imagination.

Most days America screams to anyone who'll listen how it hates me so much it would rather kill us all than let me live.
Home.

Our first "re-openings" are met by multiple mass shootings. We barely discuss it.

I want to cry from all the freedom.

•

Surfing a sandbar in the sea I confront what "home" means. I don't know. I'm not actually surfing, because sharks, but I confront. I sit through *Jaws*, out of doors, at least twice.

"My kids are on that beach too," its Mayor of Amity Island said, a bit over-due. He'd been mocking the sheriff for insisting they close the beaches after another deadly outbreak of shark attacks. Familiar? This time *his* kids were on the beach. This time the great white problem mattered.

"Biggest protest movement in American history" was a phrase that barely survived its own news cycle. No matter the nonstop marching, the nonstop murdering. No time to come home from a police-murder protest before another police-murder occurs.

Even in apocalyptic times, when words scarcely even mean anymore, they matter. Asian Giant Hornets become Murder Hornets become Kung Fu Virus become kids in need of a good incarceration camp.

We've needed a bigger boat, like, forever.

•

So many of us set adrift at once. Either we can't go home, or we can't leave. Crisis after crisis kick-drops all our plans. Virtuality claims even our closest family and friends. All the wrong people keep dying alone. Behind glass. Breathing plastic.

Since day drinking and night sleeping both became available choices, I've struggled to stay present through the never-ending now. I can't remember the last time I've been this still.

No flights. No road trips. No million places to be. A sweet old house by the sea where whole mammalian communities thrive between the walls like Jellicle cats.

The thing about *going*, much less *home*, is how it shrinks all the surreal, all the moments into just some things that happened. Anecdotes. Questionable, even.

•

Winter finally turns to spring sometime around midsummer on the Cape. Everything around me comes alive. Difficult as we make it, the land seems to work best it can for now. And the birds. And their songs.

I'm happy to report, for instance, that the ocean is still here. I've checked. Often. I'm thankful for the tides at least.

Another great white chomped down a seal too damned near shore the other day which I know because this one not-a-stranger lady told me that's what happened.

•

Looking east from our mountain of mess to Italy's flattening curve hurts like fractured safety. So many of us saw the new world nightmare coming and tried like hell to avoid it. Again. But here we are. Krugered.

Here I am. Locked down. Tensed up. On pause. Uncertain. One whole leap-year season in exile so far with no end in sight. Spent.

A neon sign in my campus office blazes BREATHE. I miss that light. I don't know when I'll see my campus office again.

•

Everyone here wears a mask. The rare exceptions are, without exception, out-of-towners. You'd think this was Amity Island. Where did they come from? How did they get here? What have they brought? Why are they trying so hard to be strangers?

Days have begun again to take the shape of days. I look around and everyone seems to be doing things.

I'd like to do, for once, not a damned thing. But then how will I matter?
I can't always remember why these verbs become so transactional.

•

Oh, Dear.

I'd been on the road twelve weeks already by the time I landed in Rome. That far below cruising altitude, "on the road" is mostly what home has meant.

I've been anxious for months about driving again, Black, from viral coast to stubbornly viral coast. Just to land somewhere that still won't feel like home. Assuming I survive.

Then. Finally. No. I won't go.

I'll remember magic. Virtually reimagine my work. Embrace this gifted corner by the sea. Remain thrown away and netted and held and fortunate and terrified.

Everything remains unresolved.

Getting on dusk now. I think how it's always a surprise to find myself exactly where I'm supposed to be. How our lives insist on small miracles despite us.

I went to a restaurant again for the first time. I sat outside. I was as far away as everyone.

LONELINESS TOO

With a deep ache ♩ = 48

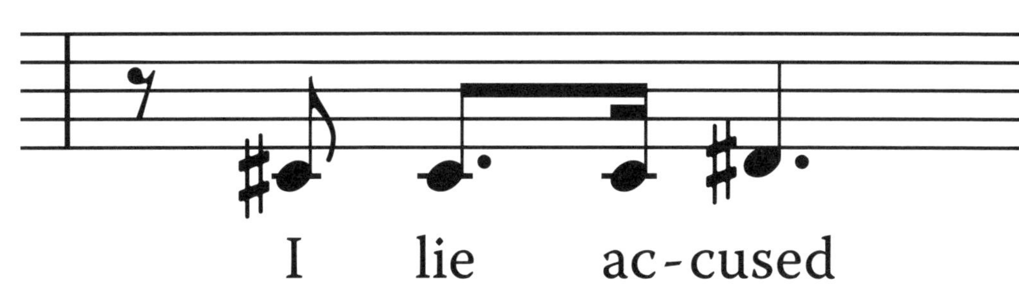

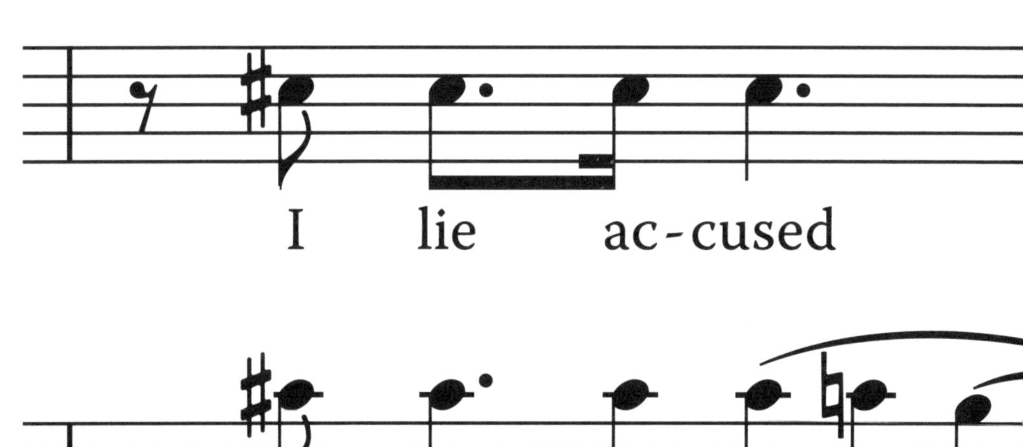

I lie ac - cused_____

Lately I've struggled
Everything can seem a lie
no one really seems alive anymore
Do we ever even notice outside?
Seems there's nothing left but feeling.

mf *p*

No thought. No action. Just Paralysis.
And feeling. Tuesday nearly broke me.
I stopped believing in everything.
I stopped believing everything
I searched the night by lamplight
for my self.

Ped.

I stand accused of leaking red
old words knit to new languages
the whole world soon forgets

poco allarg. – **With clarity** ♩ = 56

66

I lie accused of bluing
with every breath I trap the air
Do I ever even notice outside?
Maybe this quiet is the star I search for myself by
When my dream's impossible
it might just take a little longer.

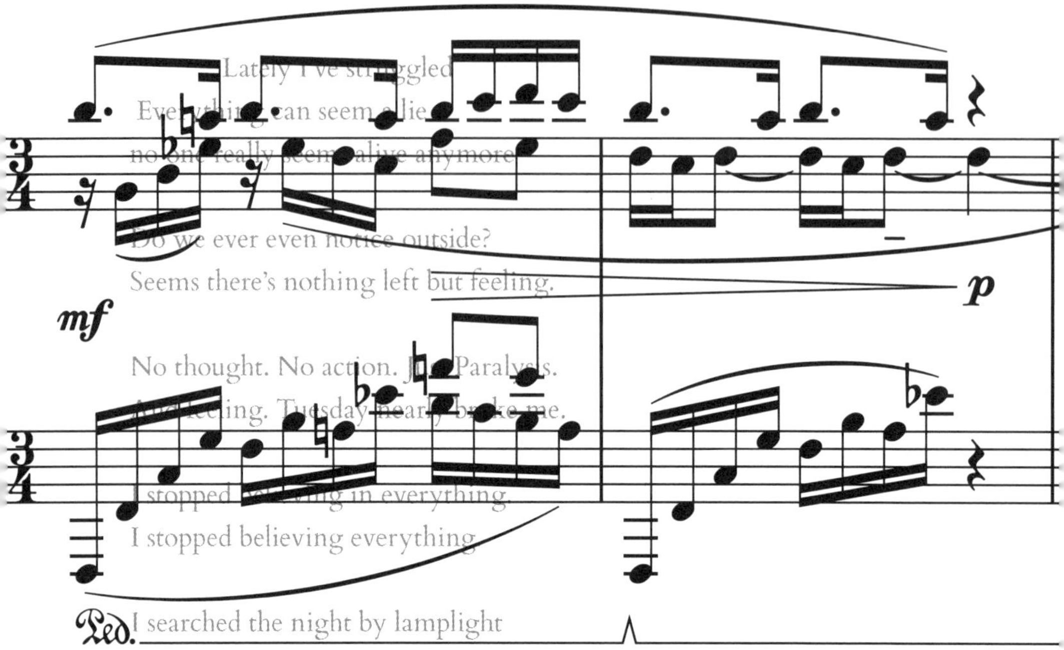

S: keep go - ing, keep go - ing, keep go - ing. *f sempre* Now!

A: keep go-ing, keep go-ing, go - ing, keep go - ing *f sempre* This is the

T: go - ing, keep go - ing, keep go - ing, go - ing, keep go - ing *f sempre* Now!

B: go - ing, keep go - ing, keep go - ing, keep go - ing *f sempre* This is the

55
lon - ger.
♩ = 64
I dream dark matters into language
soon forgotten. Some days are small miracles.
When I save my faith for faithfulness I struggle.
I rumble through sleep my like an old volcano forgotten
and my dreams fill with impossibility.
Some days insist on small miracles.
Lately I've struggled.
Some days my smallest miracle is me.
Some days the smallest miracle is keep going.
Now — This is the world we made for ourselves and —
Now — This is the world we keep on making and —
Now — maybe it's time to make something else —
Then maybe we'll dance.
Maybe I'll dance.
Dark Matters
I dream these dark mat-ters through lan-guage I too soon for - - get, for
a tempo
I stopped be - liev - - - ing in
e - - - - - - - - - very - - thing.
Dark M
18
S
T
broke me

SOLO AUTHOR

=

CONCEPTUAL BOOBY TRAP

picture
the truth

::

you lost

count how many times you were frightened
you remember little kindnesses
extended to you shunned cried
touched you justified scolding yourself you
didn't want children you began to reason
thus

::

you didn't like children because as always
daughters busied themselves as women caring

for infants with broken hearts
as though they were little girls

in retrospect part of you admired these girls
from a distance anyway climbing up
a wall or basking in the sun the life-
giving aspects interested you you once said it
was the visceral dislike of children's babble
their mechanical contrivances the
noise demands the surprise listening to you
suffering from some complaint you had no
name for

THANKS MR. KAUFMAN

who not-failed me in first-semester geometry—
he's dead so he can't ♥ this—and

i'll thank the great lesbian who brought me—light!—
up to the top grade in second-term geometry—
who taught the living-ass hell outta all that area—
and didn't even mind my mouth

i mean
imagine
somehow the man
still gets top billing

even here
in my own mouth

i mean imagine then how
my life could matter

i mean not like someone else's but like
enough—it's not exactly a given is it

what with all the planes
and dimensions and directionality

which all lead me straight to velocity—
of course—American—
but this is where my highways roam

where we jones toward blown
quarks and so there it is and

there i am : congruent : complicit :

proof

GREENWICH MEANS

pressured
forced—shoved
from what is to
what should

enemy of presence
carrier of stress
illness delivery system

like something that came
with slavery like a lie
we insist on

an old tomorrow
another yesterday

not always on time not always
when called not
an appointment

anti-response to presence

opposite
o'clock

but you are an adult (surely)
what you didn't say whatever it was worth you
knew when bedrooms closed sleeping lids
when their tongues tasted staleness in
their mouths their parents surrendered
in bed when thoughts were unharnessed
and allowed to roam freely (you knew)
you could tell stories no one was listening to
(to(o))
in the late hour in the night's darkness
you allow the adult to emerge
express adult thoughts
and then the two of you like adults
exchange (secrets)
condemn and pass judgments talk
about (daily) blood-letting

LESSONS LEARN

D FROM SHAME:

PHLEGETHON

say
                    drown

mean
                    burn

mean
                    solve for

                              self

can't

          can't

                      don't

hold tight

               let go

let go
                    let—

You ate ten times as much
at four-and-a-half weighed a ton
nicknamed Monster hearing mother say ::

wHY hAVE yOU mADE mE a mONSTER?

::
(wHY
hAVE yOU
mADE mE a
mONSTER?)
::

You tell the story but suddenly features change
expression (that's enough)

(change the subject to something trivial) tell a story
until your breathing slows shallows knee-
highs Mothers

were generally indulgent first
then ruthlessly rigid strict

You imagined constant loss all the time
instructed (women) in their best tottered past them

some can afford indulgence
some see angels and marvel
some have no children and are thus blessed
many admire adults who admire
them

So I wake up to news that they took Sid to the Düsseldorf emergency room in the middle of the night.

I'm not being honest about something. It only took two sentences to lie.

Enough about me—more about me:

Here's where I'm Pinocchio-stuck: I keep thinking about how we ask our friends for help. Now my chest hurts when I think about it almost as much as it hurts when I ask for help. And still I think: what blessing. I imagine being so accustomed to care and support, love and attention, to know that not only are you deserving of help but that people love you and that people who love you will also, in fact, help you (someone wise-hearted here would say that they even "want to help you").

Then I imagine my own mother: going to her in the middle of the night, sick, to tell her that I'd found an emergency room close by, to ask if she can help me get there. This is the scene I see:

MOM: "You know where the keys are."

ME: "But I'm feeling weak, dizzy, feverish . . ."
OR JUST: "Can you come with me?"

MOM: [Long rant about how tired she is, how much work she has, how early she has to be up, and how no one ever takes her work seriously . . .]

So, whatever. Back to me, of course. Am I not my mother's daughter?

Something about fairy tales like *Beauty and the Beast* (always one and the same), and all that business with frog kissing, makes a dream mind think: If one is Monster, can one really be made lovable by the love of another?

Is that all I'm missing? Love? If I had love, would I stop being Monster?

Could I then, nose unstretched, become Real Girl?

ALMOST SURE

THERE'S A

MORE

HATEFUL

STARE

BUT ALSO

NOT AT ALL SURE

WABENZI WALKS

because voices
like bodies shadow

linger and
are torn apart
and linger

are torn
apart and
linger like

the thousand eyes of night:
a scorpion
a Cuyahoga
a river
burns awake

cries that were the mom
not the kid but—wait—
(we are) not a fairy tale

even fairies
fail our families
some times
some wheres

WHY DID YOU LEAVE?

years ago, Metric's
"Combat Baby" was all over

my facefeed—at the time
it was right on
time and all I wanted was to remain
unlooked at   even today   sort of
just like other people.   Here's
the thing:

I don't want to hold onto
you, dear   I don't
even want to hold you

why should I?
HAVE YOU SEEN ME?!?
lucky, lucky

though I hope you are held
—well—just—also—

POINT OF PRIVILEGE!
says the board of directors
directing all the women
how to brush their hair
in mirrors on film

WHY DIDN'T YOU LEAVE?

low-priced
luxury goods

[click like]
but—wait—

no kings
no horses

—ideally—
no men

[fire emoji]
we eat ourselves

until we're gone
well I do—how

'bout you?
[fire emoji]

and the colored girls click
like like like like like like like like
like like like like like like like like
like like like like like like like like
like like like like like like like like
like
[frowny face emoji]

see me
I'm listening
here
you are
(yes you)
here

a night flight lit
(from) my fire

asleep while
I need
to dance

look at you
[fire emoji]

you
here you
*cut "are"
hear me?

sssssshhhhh—
listen
(repeat)

[footsteps]

sssssshhhhh—
listen
(repeat)

go quiet. know
something's 'bouta happen:
respond or pay it no nevermind.

  also the Central Park parrots: fancy, unlike
  the city-old elite messenger pigeons: abandoned
  to the street. to our days-old bread.

  also how italians say *crow*.
  also these seagulls —
    evil-ass ocean geese. also
    us
    atwirl.

botheredly unbothered
we step over each other.

we are all out
of days-old bread.

BY NIGHT

YOU'RE REALLY FAITHFUL TO YOUR ABUSERS, AREN'T YOU?

Like love: first you pick up; then you lay down; then discard; then discard; then discard. That's love. Right? Did somebody say Dominoes? The problem of a street game is you. You're already doing it wrong. Doing it wrong before you wake up. Before you walk up the street. Cross the crowded corner. Case in point: When you reach the bones table, you stop. Stare. Consider. Count. Think: this is a lovely afternoon for a friendly game of dominoes! Call next. Figure they don't hear. Call next again. You call louder. You call in Spanish. Then you walk (again, with the walking) into the bodega. Come out with four 40 oz bottles. Suddenly somebody hears. Suddenly the smell of holes burning pockets. Suddenly, the game you watch ends. Like love. Right? Somebody?

ENTITLEMENT

LANGUAGE

HURRY UP, PLEASE, IT'S CLOSING TIME

I. "TIPPECANOE & TYLER TOO!"

> Lately, I've become accustomed to the way
> The ground opens up and envelops me
> —AMIRI BARAKA / LEROI JONES
> "Preface to a Twenty Volume Suicide Note"

Same.

And something about what Jeanette Winterson called art anticipating life. About streets tinged with the ancient dangers we pose to each other. Everyone's a stranger now in a world at war for years with no end in sight. East Asia. Eurasia. We all know the active-shooter drill.

A full score, plus two, years into the 21st century and the 20th still haunts our everyday, popping up around corner after corner with the jolt of a Roland Emmerich *bwah*. But let me hurry this up, please, because this is America. The haunting goes back far and deep and us floating through year two of a lifeguard shortage. To wit:

It's been said (or, is about to be) that the very long century preceding the century-ago publication of T.S. Eliot's "The Waste Land" was presaged by a powerful omen. There. I just said it. Look up the Battle of Tippecanoe, as direct a lead-up to the colony-clashing, Indigenous-slaughtering War of 1812 as Ferdinand's assassination another century hence would be to World War I, and you'll likely learn of William Henry Harrison's seminal *(ew)* victory. Major general, legionnaire, then-governor of the so-called Indiana Territory, and the new nation's soon-to-be 9th president, Harrison dined out on those war stories, from river to coast, one can imagine, for decades.

In truth, the battle was more of a draw.

Therein lies the power of a sticky line. Harrison is credited as the first US president to employ modern campaign tactics in the run for the role of his life. "Tippecanoe and Tyler Too" was among the nation's first electoral slogans. You can almost smell the merch paste slapping Harrison's infamous moniker next to the alliterative surname of his running mate. Nearly thirty years after Tecumseh's War and the death of the infamous warrior, his brother, Tenskwatawa "the Shawnee Prophet," cursed the American presidency. Harrison—the shortest-serving president in US history—died. Only thirty-one days post-inauguration, Harrison was the first. He wouldn't be the last.

Call it a myth. Call it the thing itself. Call it the Twenty-Year Curse. Or Tecumseh's Curse. It's been called the Curse of Tippecanoe, called Curse Zero too. Legend has it the curse promised every future president elected during a year which ends in zero would die in office. My mother, who survived the 1960s, referred to this with astonishing frequency.

This rule of zero would come to pass every twenty years. Each settling a score. This spell-bound carnage lasted a score and a century more until suddenly—right before my own child eyes, glued to a milk-truck-sized color teevee—it didn't. I sat mesmerized and confused as Reagan took six bullets, again and again on replay, and then kind of . . . walked away?

Teflon Ron they called him; and all the way up through Defcon Don the shattered curse blew right through a man who knew to duck a shoe—experience or instinct—which flew line-true right by his head. Undead? Nearly four score years have passed since the last potentially cursed presidential passing. President Biden, next up on the Curse Zero schedule, hosted COVID chest-tight at least twice and well . . . undead?

To a woman, everyone to whom I mentioned writing about Eliot's "The Waste Land" broke into laughter. "Like," their dancing eyes asked, "why?!"

Look around. Centuries ago, a Roman army's century contained around four score legionnaires. "Things have come," Baraka prefaced, "to that."

II. "I AM GOD, LA DE DAH."

—ANNE SEXTON
"Hurry Up Please It's Time"

It was December 31, 2005, and the *New York Times* opined through poetry, opening its pages to poets, including Brigit Pegeen Kelly's consummate prose poem, "Closing Time; Iskandariya," alongside work by Carl Phillips, Seamus Heaney, and Yusef Komunyakaa. Two years had passed since thousands of priceless cultural artifacts were looted from Baghdad and thousands upon thousands of even more priceless humans had been killed.

"It was not a scorpion," began Kelly's first epic sentence, its word count nearly nine-score long. "I asked for a fish," she continued, "but maybe God misheard my request." A fortnight prior to the poem's publication, which unlike "The Waste Land" has never been collected in book form, Dubya finally conceded that his pre-war Iraqi intelligence "turned out to be wrong." Eighty-three Decembers had passed since "The Waste Land" crossed the ocean; Dubya continued to insist that his war was justified. His war would continue for six more years.

So what of Kelly's desert creature? Its exoskeleton? Its poison barb? In what ways was it "a thing like me?" Or, perhaps, like us, innocently cruel in our own best eyes, tripping over stiff sidesteps, "as if on ice," Kelly writes, "freezing again and again in mid-air like a listening ear." Our shells, as Baraka wrote in *Preface*'s closing poem "Notes on a Speech": "as any other sad man here / american." Tippecanoe, Indiana. Tyler, Texas. Alexandria. Babylon. Mariupol, Mogadishu, Khartoum, Jerusalem, Detroit. So many unreal cities. So many fishbones caught in our post-Lowellian throats. In 2001, a dedicated New Yorker, I was stuck across an ocean in September. Being a perhaps-problematically polite young American, I was cared for kid-glovingly before the airways profiled me all the way back to Brooklyn, whose downwinds of death finally drove me uptown. Then to Texas. New skies. Different ancestors. Then north past Tippecanoe's old air. Then, after so much long, long winding, back uptown to still-older subways. Again. Sort of. Sometimes. Because, as I regularly shudder, "they be shootin'" so . . . most times I just stay home—whatever that means.

Older even than Eliot's ordered pathos, New York's IRT shares my birthday alongside as many quietly loud roadmaps. Its Seventh Avenue line takes me home again, after what seems a century on the highway. Its tracks, and perhaps some of its train cars, turned eighteen years old—grown!—just as Eliot first published "The Waste Land" in the UK, a fistful of weeks before it came home.

In John Beer's 2010 saga, "The Waste Land," an antihero refers to Eliot as "such a shrinking violet," and Beer quips, "thank God, we live in a day and age / where people aren't afraid to talk about orgasms." In truth, in our century, sex has become so antediluvian: an unreal city littered with outdated maps. The end of sex hadn't been printed—I've been taught by global trauma to note—on my end-of-the-world-bingo-card. But here we are.

III. "NOBODY SINGS ANYMORE."

—AMIRI BARAKA / LEROI JONES,
"Preface to a Twenty Volume Suicide Note"

Chaos sings though.

> It is February 7th, 1979. The sky is blue-gold:
> the freedom of possibility.
> —FATIMAH ASGHAR
> "Pluto Shits on the Universe"

The angry these days say, page after page, that our songs aren't music. But what of the fear that our music may be magic?

"I chaos," promises Asghar's Pluto, "like a motherfucker."

According to my phone, ninety-nine years after Eliot published "The Waste Land," a 72-year-old Indian news outlet asked, "Why does the U.S. lose all its wars?"

This morning, across a workshop table, a woman spoke of her impending evening Bible Study: "We're doing prophecy." She won't write that poem though. I tried.

Gregg Bordowitz once described his "Debris Fields" poems to me as "literally . . . wreckage."

> FATIGUE SADNESS DREAD CALENDAR SCHEDULE
> ROUTINE HABIT DISCOMFORT BOREDOM GRIPE
> ANTICIPATION VISITOR LOVER
> EXCITEMENT ANXIETY SENSES
> PEONIES PETALS FALL MORTALITY
> VANITAS INEVITABILITY
> —GREGG BORDOWITZ
> "Debris Fields V"

In 2018—the Late Before Times—I made this poem into a broadside. Its insistent dive into the wreck threatened to drown—its vanitas, inevitable even then.

IV. "CHAOS ISN'T A PIT," OPINED GEORGE R.R. MARTIN'S PETYR BAELISH, BUT NOT IN THE BOOK. "CHAOS IS A LADDER."

> "The ladder is always there
> . . .
> We know what it is for,
> we who have used it."
> —ADRIENNE RICH
> "Diving Into the Wreck"

By the time you read this, I assume we'll have been great again for quite some time.

Today my watch says: August 4, 2022. One or another deadly heat dome hovers, my watch says.

The rats in Manhattan are bolder now—one tried to drag its slimy belly right across my shoe the other day. There was a witness.

We either are or are not at war right now. Could it all have become the same thing? Mostly though there is no water.

And today a student talked about going into poetry for the money and I laughed. I mean, I was wearing Gucci, but I was hungry. Unfed. And I laughed.

All the fancy shoes in the world have yet to secure me the transactional skills of an Eliot publishing a poem across a pond. Offered a full month's (pandemic-dipped, to be fair) 21st-century Manhattan rent as honorarium to publish the poem, Eliot was offended. I imagine a pearl clutch. I imagine how Beer's poem pegs its fifth and final section as "The Death of the Poet." May we all have an ol' buddy like Ezra Pound to slice the fat off our meaty poems and swaddle up a hefty poetry award prize purse to sweeten the deal. To inject that fat into the wallets of the poet and his publishers. In the end: money and money. And yeah, war. And horror. And money.

In the end, even Maurizio Gucci got shot down in the '90s, as if some ordinary American.

An ordinary-enough American, I've been on the highway, poeming, all summer, and even my sUbLeTteR fled the scaffold-dark and heat of my August flat. Apparently some man was pissing himself on my doorstep.

No one watered my plants the rest of the sun-hot summer.

V. "IN THE FAINT MOONLIGHT, THE GRASS IS SINGING"

> —T.S. ELIOT
> "The Waste Land"

> The trouble with being a woman, Skeezix,
> is being a little girl in the first place.
> —ANNE SEXTON
> "Hurry Up Please It's Time"

Twenty-five years to the day after Eliot's death I called myself reborn at the Los Angeles Airport's Tom Bradley International Terminal. Grown. Finally. Free.

I stayed through the riots and then struck north to apprentice myself to poetry like Kelly's maudlin lover. "[A] house of books, my shy scorpion, carrying in his belly all the perishable manuscripts," and it was me, "a little mirror of the library at Alexandria, which burned."

"Preface to a Twenty Volume Suicide Note" ends with the speaker's young daughter praying—ostensibly to no one—for our salvation. Black women will save us all! I hear the preternaturally American pleurer du coeur nearly forty years after Eliot, nearly fifty years before my own home machines minted the refrain into light-sound.

In 1980, the year Reagan won his (undead?) office, June Jordan wrote "From Sea to Shining Sea." Such vanitas! Such inevitability! Her epicacious, seven-part poem lays bare our wasted and ever-wasting lands. Yet, amidst their fresh and rotten fruits she digs toward promise.

Jordan seeded the poem with single-line stanzas which stated plainly all the things that "This was not a good time" to be: Black; gay; woman; young; old; Arkansan; a pomegranate ripening on a tree.

In the poem's fifth section, Jordan prophesizes:

> Natural order is being restored.
> Designer jeans will be replaced by the designer
> of the jeans.
> Music will be replaced by reproduction
> of the music.
> Food will be replaced by information.
> Above all the flag will be replaced by the flag.

And Reagan lived. And Trump got his very own flag; they pass me still down every highway, flapping ominous, all a-glare, red font bursting mid-air. Somewhere in the middle distance, a president covered his cough all summer as I worked on an erasure of Langston Hughes's "Let America Be America

Again." To pull from beneath his poem long, cruel months of poetry felt found and true to me.

We may be tempted to imagine that Jordan's poem might end as an embodiment of Baraka's Black girl in prayer but, to echo Asghar's Pluto, "Nah." Jordan knew exactly to whom she spoke. Her poem is direct address and insistent call to action.

Action? Here?

In these post-Lowellian lands where Eliot might look around and note the lack of floodless waters? The way our days may only be rock but still somehow they burn? Such vanitas. Such inevitability.

> Today, I broke your solar system. Oops.
>
> —FATIMAH ASGHAR
>
> "Pluto Shits on the Universe"

"Shanti," Eliot purloined. "Shanti. Shanti."

Action:

Shall we at least set our wasted lands in order? Can we hurry up, please? Can we track losing time in our surveilling rear view?

Or do we continue to channel Asghar's Pluto and hold tight its stubborn answer, "Nah."

Shanti. Shanti. Shanti.

Ugh.

Om.

HYPER PALATABL

PALATABLI

NOT PALATABLI

HOW TO SWING

darkness

you see me here
where mosquitos go during daylight

See me! I'm
right here! raised

by wolves to be some Tarzan's
vine-bound Jane Porter

I almost ate myself
until I was gone and

still
somehow

empire

call this place
my home

ungrounded
unfound
(ed?) civility lost

meet my

half land
    half city
all sea

swallow my
light

HOW NOT TO STAY UNSHOT IN THE U.S.A.

EAT GARLIC. GO TO ELEMENTARY SCHOOL
POP STAR SING. SEE A MOVIE. TEACH CREAT
ERS BUT BLACK. ATTEND MIDDLE SCHOOL. A
FROM THEIR CAR SPEAKERS IF BLACK. SWIM
BUT BLACK. SHOP. BE BLACK, BUT THAT'S
SCHOOL. BE FROM THE STATES. BE FROM AN
PLAY INSIDE. HAVE A GUN. HAVE BIBLE STU
A PARTY. BE GAY. BE STRAIGHT. GO TO WOR
BAR. GO TO THE BEACH. HAVE WAFFLES WH
BASICALLY BE ANYWHERE NEAR AN AIRPOR
AND MAYBE WANNA NOT BE PREGNANT. GO
STOP FOR GAS. SUPERMARKET SHOPPING. BE
SERVE AN ORDER OF PROTECTION. JOIN TH
GO TO TEMPLE. STOP AND GET A COFFEE. LI
POLICE IN AN EMERGENCY. GO TO CHURCH.
A PARENT. BREAK UP WITH SOMEONE. HAV
TV WITH FAMILY. TEACH IN ANY SCHOOL,
THUS MAKING SOMEONE SAD. BE MAYBE JUS
BE SOMEONE'S GIRLFRIEND. MAKE NEWSPAP
AT THE CLUB. GO TO THE BANK. WRITE. BE
SAFE? GO TO COURT. BE SOMEONE'S WIFE. RO
AND/OR FOOD. ATTEND YOUR WORKPLAC
NEED YOUR NEIGHBOR. CONGRESS. DRIVE
SITTING IN THEIR INTERNATIONAL HOUSE
SOMEWHERE ELSE. GET A BOOK FROM THE L
BE A DOCTOR. NATIONAL INTELLIGENCE. G
MOSQUE. BE A COP. IMMIGRATE. HAVE OR B
SELL CARS. MCCHILL. WANT SOME CHICK
HOTEL. SHARE SOME FRO-YO. WALK DOWN
A DORMITORY. HOMECOMING. HANDLE YO
TO THE PARKING LOT. FIND YOURSELF IN
IN AN APARTMENT. LIVE OFF THE RESERVA
RUN BY A GIANT MOUSE. SEEK CUSTODY OF
CHOW MEIN. TRADE STOCKS. SAY "MA'AM,
AT A WENDY'S. ANCHOR THE TV NEWS. DAT
REALLY. RUN OUT OF GAS. HAVE A CHILD.

TO A COUNTRY MUSIC FESTIVAL. GO SEE A
VRITING. PLAY LOUD MUSIC ON CAR SPEAK-
OMEONE ABOUT THE LOUD MUSIC COMING
BLACK. LAY ABOUT A POOL NOT SWIMMING
NEW. BE WHITE. BE AT HOME. BE IN HIGH
HERE ELSE. GO TO TEMPLE. PLAY OUTSIDE
DON'T HAVE A GUN. JOIN THE ARMY. HAVE
ATCH FOOTBALL. PLAY SPORTS. GO TO THE
THEY HAVE A HOUSE. MAKE SOCIAL MEDIA
SIT THE MALL. BE A VETERAN. BE PREGNANT
SLEEP IN YOUR OWN BED. GO TO CHURCH
URSE. BE A COLLEGE STUDENT. AIR TRAVEL
VY. PLAY SANTA. TAKE A SPA DAY. SIGHTSEE
N THE STREETS. BE A JOURNALIST. CALL THE
 SERVICE. TAKE THE BUS. BE A PARENT. HAVE
FAMILY. BE ALONE. TAKE AN UBER. WATCH
WHERE. ANSWER YOUR FRONT DOOR. DIE
LITTLE BIT CRAZY, NO HARM. BE A MARINE
HELP. GO TO GRADUATE SCHOOL. DANCING
KEN HOSTAGE, WHICH USED TO BE KIND OF
YOUR NEIGHBORHOOD. DELIVER PACKAGES
RAINING. HAVE EITHER WALLS OR DOORS
AR. BE A NEIGHBOR. EAT PANCAKES WHILE
A REFUGEE, HAVING ESCAPED BEING SHOT
ARY. PAUSE AT A REST STOP, HOPING TO REST
O THE PARK. TAKE THE TRAIN. ATTEND THE
N IN-LAW. PROTEST. WALK ACROSS CAMPUS
BE A PATIENT. BE A SECRETARY. STAY IN A
STREET. LIVE ON THE RESERVATION. STAY IN
POST OFFICE BUSINESS. RUN FOR OFFICE. GO
ERATE NEED OF HELP. EAT ICE CREAM. LIVE
N. HUNT. TAKE THE KIDS TO A PIZZA SHOP
UR CHILDREN. GO TO LAW SCHOOL. CRAVE
IS A WENDY'S" BECAUSE YOU ARE, INDEED
KE, ANYONE REALLY. MARRY, LIKE, ANYONE
A CHILD. LIVE IN A HOUSE. LOVE A CHILD

STYX

measure

    weight

measure

        heft

penny a pound

who will remember

you   animal

  you   meat

do you deserve

this kind death?

answer me

                ssssssshhhhhhhhhh

answer me

NEGRO BEING :

say I . gender unclear . gender unclear . go ahead . stare . No, wait, that would be on opposite
aring. clearly your very first time seeing a real live Negro. Congratulations! How wonderful fo
es, we are freakishly beautiful, we know . feel free to express your absolute joy and gratitude at
ne . Number three, go ahead and laugh, why not? We as a people are hilarious. There's room
eautiful. Is just fine, thank you . And finally, number five, you're going to like this one. Go ahe
ile. Laugh with, not at. Am I laughing? No, stop it. Just stop it. I didn't see you there. your
ould be on opposite. Don't stare. That's rude as fuck. I didn't see you there staring . assure yo
otentially the greatest day of your life occurs on animals. Well, yes, we are freakishly beautiful.
at. Try to keep it together . go ahead and stare, oh, no, wait, that would be an opposite day, w
ant to fuck this up. Go ahead and , wait, that would be on opposite . Don't do that, kid. It's fu
r now. I'm going to go back to the very important business of being my Black ass, hope you e
ou're right to feel it. Number four, why, yes. feel free to express your absolute joy and gratitude
o. Tell your friends, be excited. We aren't. and finally, number five, you're really gonna . Five
our friends want to . You are beautiful. Is just fine, thank you. Their day's coming have them
ght to feel it. Just don't spaz out on us, we're likely in the middle of something very, very imp
al, real, real, real. Now . There's room for us all . Just remember the platinum rule. Laugh wit
feel it. Just don't spaz . In fact, I'm in the middle of saving the world again . Help your friend
o go ahead and stare, no, wait, that would be an opposite day —(Don't staircase that Chatswo
o. Now go. Tell your friends, be excited. We aren't. We are real. We are amazing. Well, that's a
are. Number two, do not touch. Now, this one is really serious . Go ahead and stare. All that e
cking rude. In fact, we're probably busy doing something very important, like saving the wor
together, really. Help your friends . Hold on to it. don't fuck it up . Am I laughing? Am I laug

ch it most assuredly is not. Don't stare, really. Don't do that. It's rude dude. I didn't see you the
st remember, always laugh with, not at. assure your own joy on this great day. number four, wh
rtunity to view our countenance . Beyond that try not to spaz out on us . You're beautiful is ju
. Just remember, always laugh with, not at . assure your own success on this great day . You a
pread tale of your great fortune. Negroes are real. You know, what? Just remember the platinu
real live Negro. What a day for you. I'm here to help you with your success. No, wait. No, th
uccess on this great day. Number two, do not touch. Now, this one is really serious, even if th
to express your excitement and actual gratitude at the opportunity to . Opportunity to . Beyon
most assuredly . Help your friends. Their day is coming soon, and they, like you, probably don
le. And with that, congratulations, your first real live Negro, isn't it a gas? Well, that's all for r
t. Watch it again. Hold on to it. We are real. We are amazing. All that excitement, you feel we
pportunity to view our countenance. Your beautiful is just fine . Try not to spaz out on us . No
really gonna go ahead spread the tale of your great fortune . Just remember, always laugh wit
y probably don't want to fuck this up . like you . All that excitement, you feel, well, you'
ke saving the world again. And number five, is possibly gonna to be your favorite. Negroes a
. No, no, I'm not laughing. So stop it, just stop . We're amazing. All that excitement you're rig
day is coming soon. And they, like you, probably don't want to buy this . Go ahead and laug
to keep it together. Help your finally first real live Negro! isn't it a gas? don't want to fuck th
I'm going back to the very important business of being my Black ass. What a day for you. do
t, you feel well, No, wait, that would be on opposite day. We're amazing. Don't do that, kid. I
. All that excitement? you're right to feel it. You are beautiful, is just fine, thank you. try to ke
Vatch it again. Am I laughing? Am I laughing? Hold on . [Empty]

BEING A "NEGRO FIRST" FEELS SO LAST CENTURY

blah blah blah
there was a plague.
again. gwen called it

better than the alternative:
to live. you'd never know
so many of us do. despite ourselves
everyone has a story. when june asked
what we should do those of us who
did not die i imagine what she'd say
if i answered: lie around drunk and bake
bread; make cookies; never quite spread
the tight space that crushes us.

put my foot in the grass. press
toward grounding. pull back flesh
like hot ice. on the boiled side of melt.
it was cold it was hot it blazed
and that was before the never-
ending today of plague ran viral.
everywhere people with all
the anger all the guns feel outnumbered.
listen: they are. Still

i guess we're just supposed to talk
about all this bullshit now. but

the leaves this autumn: incredible!
how they too flaunt flames deep

into december like they know
how fast we forget our own spilled
blood. walk beneath the canopy of me. see how
i hover how i don't so much block light as scatter light
how i kitten yarn batter light. as fofie would say
if for just one day we didn't have to earn
for just one day then who do we (want
to) become? brown and green and recent
rainwet sets everything alight like
the untoward way raindrops flash and prick
each bit of waning sunlight when i come back
around and meet myself after all this baking
in the new dark—do i just assume, june, that
i can remember to swim or let the current
pull me down again? here we insist
today did not happen here through
all of today's happenings here.

tfw you know horrible things happened
but you can't remember them

tfw you remember horrible thing after horrible thing
and still you think: nope—that's not the one

tfw there's nothing left but feeling—
no thought—just paralysis—and feeling

tfw there's nothing left to feel
and nothing in the lap for breakfast

so it turns out i'm allergic to society
as a whole. when in doubt, they say,

go back in time. when i wanna feel safe
i figure i should want something else.
everywhere i go everyone i see could be
a shooter and my breasts beneath
bulletproof vests squeeze the breath outta
me. tomorrow may be another country but

even there the philosopher's
stone ain't stone: bottoms out
unexpectedly. i can't forget water

while i drown so why does today's silence
engulf so unseen and unsmelled and even
then tomorrow is not even there. maybe
this quiet is a star. our outer space treaties
are older now than my whole
generation. just as outdated.
just as orbited by garbage and left
to rot with our every epizootic breath.

it is, our leaders—*ha?*—*hee?*—say, what
it is.

in rome i had a red feather boa.
i'd tickle your nose with my loosey-
goosey feathers. i ruled the stage, honey.
long gone now, but then? how i blazed.

STUPID
AVERAGE
BORING
HUMDRUM
EVERYDAY
NUMBNESS

OF THE END OF US

UNTIE

no one pulls your coat, when you're impossibly young, that your green scarf—the one with the abstract camo print which you'll buy some summer saturday as you stroll alongside a love interest who has no interest—will be worn, barring tragedy, for the next thirty years. that, since it's never been lovely enough to lose or pair, it's nearly always clean. that for the next thirty

years, there that scarf will be. its same shifting greens that airport agents
mushed their hands all over, held up the angry line,
to remove: to expose

beneath my pin curls. my curl pins
never remained silent again. you're not
warned of such unending noise
when you're young or
are you?

that pin can stick you into situations
no one mentioned would never be in your control, or would
—nor were you warned of the inevitability of this shrinkage, this
suffocation of air that used still to smell of night jasmine past noon but now?

now? taste it. metallic.
rancid with fear.

how impossible to anticipate thirty years even after you've lived them.

even after you've lived them again, imagine. you'd lost
that old, tattered scarf by then. long ago, probably, or never will—forget

that summer saturday unrequited. even if right here, here,

lies someone you love. unimaginably young. let me pull your coat:
resist the pull toward silence, slouching, abstract, camo'd green.
when reminded to remember, instead the love? well—
remember, instead, the love.

I

RAW

NAKED

AN

UNBURIED

BULB

WHO'S OSMOSIN' WHO

After Ernie Barnes' The Sugar Shack *(1976)*

suddenly, Uncle say, but—

say
  I keep looking at these two women up top—and then Uncle points—I mean
    points to just the place in the painting
I'd circled
just the spot I'd been dreaming on for months
I asked
You see two women? dancing?

then, Yeah—then—You know—this one? then finger-wags the one in heels and starts to explain that he thinks she's a woman and I'm like:

quiet. listening. it's the way—as the data farms say—that
the one most marked femme is who Uncle explains
for me.   the way the gerrymandered geographies of gender marking are removed—replaced—unidentified. and then, intuition exposed—Uncle bashfuls himself a bit.

Uncle—not a bashful man—bashfuls a bit and says well, says

—I don't know—

through prodding switchbacks of thought—says: it's just—it's
relative, I guess. and Cousin, the deejay, hears music. sees geometry all in all through the mask-shaft of diamond light—its isosceles sunbeam beyond the point for two women midstep.

Just then Aunt strolls through the room's assumed equilaterality, with a moving squint at the scene and shouts

Joy!

and starts dancing. Dancing! Aunt *was* that painting's party. together, her movements said, we can be—we are—us two women. those two men talkin'

'bout that nigga zoomin' his head in the corner.
still sullen
understage. perched
outside the light.
by now the only one
not dancing.

where a nigga find that chair?

I think that's a white guy, someone said.
yeah, someone said. that's a white man.

SO PREPARED FOR

DISAPPOINTMENT

SO MAD AT

SATISFACTION

LIKE

AM I

SUPPOSED TO DO

WITH THIS?

:: lists ::

genres
not-genres

survival
surveillance

:: lists ::

bath salts
meds
nail stuff
grapefruit juice
keys
protein
tequila
other keys
gin
grapefruit juice
other other keys
hair

:: lists ::

things i won't be answering:
emails

voicemails
really any mail without a stamp
phone calls
call outs
call ins
ungrounded theories
anything that begins "can i touch . . ."

:: states ::

potentially
pointless

surveillance
survival

:: states ::

selfish
she invites
all the curses
(no curse for you!)

:: states ::

how are we all so busy now
again

:: lists ::

my name
the way my name
is said

yawn

THANK YOU

s ssssss ssssss ssssss ssssss sssssoooooooooooooooooooo

o o o o o o o o o o o o o o o o o o o o o o o o o o o o o o o o o

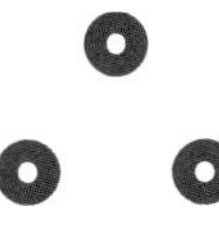

oooooooooooooooooooooooooooooooooooooooooooooooooooooooo

oooo o o o o o o o o o o o o o o o o o o o o o o o o o o o o o o o o o o o

o oooooooo oooooo ooooo ooooooo oooooooo

o oooooooo oooooo ooooo ooooooo oooooooo

oooooooooooooooooooooooooooooooooooooooooooooooooooooooo

oooo o o o o o o o o o o o o o o o o o o o o o o o o o o o o o o o o o o o

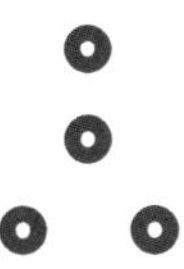

o oooooooo oooooo ooooo ooooooo ooooooooo

Numb of soul. **You are not yourself.** Anyway. When your uncle speaks. On your behalf. **Wonder.** of friends. (creatures of fiction) Whose **likes** and dislikes. Are a **blood** relation. Large. Large. (secret) Doubt. You were given birth to by notions formulated in heads. **Yes.** Question yourself. **Question** all those who meet you. Sit. Sleepless. **Drop.** Conjure. **Fly.**

Exist. Think. Yes that's the word. That is not the heavens. Unless there are. Unless. **You were not a child.** Breathing just like anybody else. Leap to the tongue. The way blind eyes tend to. Numerous **doorways. Solid** and prominent. **Are enabled.** Through forests. Without any clearing.

Ceased to exist as beings prodigious imagination. Journeys to a region. **In the wake** of the old man. There was a girl. a butcher. Stone steps too numerous to count. **In the wake** of the old man. **There was a girl.** A butcher. [breathe] **In the wake** of the old man. There was a girl. [breathe] A butcher. In the wake of the old man. There was a girl. [breathe] **A butcher.** Knowing [breathe] what knives of destiny a**wait** [breathe].

> "... there is indeed a great force in the world, a force spiritual and able to shape the physical universe, but that force is not something cut off, not something separate from ourselves. It is the energy in us, the strongest in our working, breathing, thinking together as one people; weakest when we are scattered, confused, broken into individual, unconnected fragments."
>
> —AYI KWEI ARMAH

I've always been a night person. Me, in this body, since I entered it: a night person. My early memories include nights with my pops—partners in starshine. The two of us up until even the teevee went to bed. I remember the bars that blazed onscreen. The anachronistically unmolested star-spangled banner. The snow saying: Psssshhh. You. Go. Sleep.

Pops and I watched all manner of strange. This news. That news. Wacky late-night programming and public teevee documentaries. One heavy memory: an ever-invading swarm. "Aggressive and belligerent," *National Geographic* warned, "Africanized bees, sometimes called killer bees."

My father, the African human, rolled his eyes. But me? The Africanized? The child wondering what words might mean? The language sung with the promise of stung.

So many of those movies—from the 70s, 80s, 90s, beyond—are all the same film really:

> "A storm gathers on the horizon."
> "An invasion decades in the making."

It's easy to forget who they're talking about—or to remember.

> "An alien species is staking claim to the Americas."

> “Creatures that would die rather than retreat.”
>
> “The result of a single experiment—an experiment that went terribly wrong.”

Insert SLAVERY. Insert BLACK. Insert COLONIALISM. Insert GENOCIDE. Insert OTHER. Insert ME. Be afraid, the television always says. Surely then. Surely now.

Always a new killer. Always a new violence. The swarm of it. And I keep receiving the same email; again and again subjected to the subject line—**Training Drill for an Active Shooter.**

Purpose of the drill: consider and practice what we would do in the event of such an incident, etcetera.

Description of the drill: Blah blah blah—The first instruction will be to “hide” (shelter-in-place) wherever you are for approximately one minute—The second instruction will be to “run” (evacuate) from the space you are in by the route you would use during an emergency. You should remain outside for approximately two minutes—The drill will conclude at approximately 11:50 a.m. Or: perhaps now; perhaps never.

In 1978 an all-star cast helmed the infamously bad fantasy film *The Swarm*. It’s easy enough to categorize as horror/hilarity except it’s not quite either. The voice-over:

> “A black mass, sir. A moving black mass.”
>
> “We have been invaded by an enemy far more lethal than any HUMAN force.”

Over a swarm of white men throwing flames from their flame throwers, the voice-over prepares us for “a story of courage . . . and sacrifice.”

"Its size is immeasurable," the disembodied voice warns.
"Its power is limitless," the disembodied voice frets.
"From now on the war against THE AFRICANS will be under military control."

Sounded familiar, even then. Pops, always a bit more lighthearted than I, on the outside at least, rolls his eyes again. Flips the page of whatever newspaper he is always reading.

But, what of me? What of us? Ridiculous fictions purport to build upon fact. How do we move through these violent contagions?

The hoops of denial continue to strangle, continue to swarm.

Outside my window, a fireworks display. Loud. Crackle and pop pop pop. For a solid twenty minutes my heart rate rises. For a solid twenty minutes I convince myself that this is, in fact, fireworks. That I needn't avoid windows. That I can keep sitting up. I know. I know but don't know—not in my body.

These days, as we crack ourselves like too-tight eggs across our shared web of digitalia, it feels more important than ever to metabolize that aggression out of our bodies and back into . . . what? To what end?

"No one was killed," said Sheron Patterson, "but a young woman was publicly disrespected by one of the police officers. He grabbed her callously, flung her bikini-clad body to the ground, pushed her face into the grass, cursed at her. She was traumatized, and so was I. The now-former public servant—who we believe should have helped her—instead had his knee in her back. Her girlfriends begged for her release. Her male companions valiantly attempt to wave towels at the officer. His response: a drawn gun. The fourteen-year-old girl I saw in the video was me."

What Patterson is saying is not metaphor. That fourteen-year-old girl *is* her. *Is* me. That trauma that is hers is mine. Is yours?

The trauma of all of us who this dangerously armed, grown man's actions frighten and silence and small. Of the continued compassionless inaction that they implicate.

But how much trauma can our bodies carry? In denying access to our grief, our ability to fully mourn (in thought, indeed in action, in a not-rush-before-the-next-horrid-tragedy), to see the other as ourselves, what have we Botoxed?

In politely wiping our tears and scrolling on, steeling ourselves for the day, well, then what? What does this arms-length relationship to grief, this allergy to the vulnerability of it blur or block or bury alive?

"The coalition emerges," Fred Moten insists to those of us who might find solace in hiding from our own implication, "out of your recognition that it's fucked up for you. In the same way that we've already recognized that it's fucked up for us. I don't need your help. I just need you to recognize that this shit is killing you too, however much more softly, you stupid motherfucker, you know?"

"In the context of tragedy," wrote June Jordan, "all polite behavior is a form of self-denial." Self-denial is itself a cultural contagion. When we are not compassionate toward each other, we are not compassionate toward ourselves. And are we not each other? We know we are. And can we not meet contagion with contagion? I know we can.

·

"I guess it was my destiny to live, but life itself compels an optimism," Jordan wrote, quoting Auschwitz survivor Elly Gross. "And what shall we do," she asked, "we who did not die? What shall we do now? How shall we grieve, and cry out loud, and face down despair?"

So, through the swarm to the hive: individually our mourning can sap us. Wrack us and wreck us. Together, as Armah wrote, our strength is magnified exponentially. Our sustainability. Our ability. What alone in our tiny, overpriced rooms lit by our blue blue screen seems impossible, well . . . keep going (remembering Claudia). Keep going.

"Either write something worth reading," Benjamin Franklin said, when he wasn't testing the light or working his slaves before petitioning on the side of freedom, "or do something worth writing."

Swarm.

One day, in Puerto Rico, the killer bees just stopped killing. No one knows why, for sure, they say, but they changed. Within just a few years the bees seemed to have become different—gentler. Some folks hypothesize that the environment plays a factor. Other folks wonder if they'd been merely outbred by the gentler honeybee—an experiment that's gone terribly right? But, no. The two bees maintain their self-same genetic distance.

The environment, though, can sing—like we can. Can feed. Can craft its own contagion and change the hive. In Puerto Rico the flowers grow so heavy and abundant for so long the hive didn't need its soldiers as much as its foragers. The hive didn't need all of that buzzcut anger and quickness-to-violence experimentally bred and let loose so the hive released it. Got not nominally free, but actually.

So can we.

"In a time of destruction," instructs Maxine Hong Kingston, "create something." Creative practice affords us the power to reclaim and restore the humanity of the living—and the dead—in both the public imaginary and in our own physical bodies, as well as in the bodies of those who engage with our work.

“Dearly beloved,” called Prince, to order, “we are gathered here today to get through this thing called life.”

We, and the bees, have no obstruction between us and the agency of our contagion. Our ability to swarm. That agency, the hive, is ours for the making.

And we are here.
And we are making.

“It is more than speculation,” promised that old *National Geographic*. “It is a prediction. The swarm is coming.”

AFTERWORD

Conceived and completed throughout the ongoing COVID-19 pandemic, *I Hope This Helps* grapples with the questions we continue to carry with us. Who will tend to us in our time of need? How do we tend to ourselves and others? What can survive the West? Rather than retreat into a fantasy realm where we don't acknowledge our collective vulnerability, Samiya slows us down to see the world and ourselves more clearly.

Amid the murky torrential waters of history, memory, and needful possibility, *I Hope This Helps* exemplifies what theorist Aliyyah I. Abdur-Rahman calls the Black avant-garde. It "gives rise to new aesthetic experiences, encourages thought restructuring, imagines alternative modes of sociality, and inspires unanticipated political interventions."[1] In this way, Samiya continues the tradition of Black study that remains curious, exciting, investigatory, imaginative, rigorous, playful, and world-expanding.

Samiya's candor grounds us as her poetics of experimentation traverse genre and medium. Poetry, prose, QR code, sculpture, video, and mixed-media woodcut prints are tools for deciphering the world we're trying to survive.

---

1. Aliyyah I. Abdur-Rahman, *Millennial Style: The Politics of Experiment in Contemporary African Diasporic Culture* (Durham: Duke University Press, 2024), 13.

Opening with a Standard[2] titled DRESSMAKER, Samiya focuses our attention on those women in cinema who show up as "actors" in stories not their own . . . in "service."

ACCOUNTANT, HANDMAID, INTERPRETER, OTHER SISTER, OTHER WOMAN, TOURIST, THE HELP

Reading these roles feels like a warning of what will happen if we continue to accept the West's violent imagination as our own. I take each Standard as a signpost, stopping me in my tracks and asking me to widen my eyes, breathe, and digest the words before me.

BEING A "NEGRO FIRST"(TM) IS SO LAST CENTURY

I read the Standards aloud, repeating each statement because it feels important to pause and reflect. I must breathe through it. Must pace myself because if I don't, I'll be swept up in celebrating the Negro First(TM) as a conclusion as opposed to a reconfiguration of the problem.

It's fitting then, that Samiya weaves history, poetry, and theory together; telling us from jump "we ain't all well" ("Per Aspera"). We're going through the motions of living but struggling to take care of ourselves. Returning to "normal" did not heal us. Quarantine kept some of us physically safe, but rebuilding our social worlds still feels like grasping for straws. We have yet to outrun the dangers that define us. Instead of telling us to run faster, work harder, and dream bigger, Samiya gives us "M A P S :: cartographies in progress" which asks us to slow down and pay attention. Linger in those encounters that shape our relationships to our bodies. This is how we way-find in the apocalypse.

After all, "black life" writes Katherine McKittrick ". . . is rebellious and always

2. See "Notes on Multimedia & Collaborative Poetries."

incomplete." It is in the ways Black women blues singers sounded migration, freedom, and desire without attaching it to a husband and children. It's also in the recovery projects by Barbara Christian, Angela Davis, Alexis De Veaux, Daphne Duval Harrison, June Jordan and, many others who understood that tracing Black women's life-worlds could not be overdetermined by scholarly discipline. Why else would Audre Lorde create her own genre? So, we can read Samiya's Standards as moments to gather ourselves, reflect, and consider next steps.

I Hope This Helps is in compelling formal company. The book finds kin alongside Robin Coste Lewis's *Voyage of the Sable Venus*, in which the poet charts a history of Black women in art, often unnamed in titles, gallery labels, or catalogs. She harnesses those non-names to story Black women's relationship to western art. Or Carrie Mae Weems's *From Here I Saw What Happened and I Cried*, in which the artist etches captions into red-tinted glass layered over photographs to expose photography's connection to Black pathology narratives. These dynamics are why Saidiya Hartman embraces the "chorus" over the singular subject to narrate the wayward lives of Black girls surviving the early-twentieth-century city, and why Fred Moten, riffing on Cedric Robinson, considers Black studies a critique of the proper. We've been here before, but not quite like this.

For Samiya, the solo author has no home here. The printed word (what she calls the "ink on tree" delivery system for her ideas) plays with artists' books, sculpture, maps, stories, memories, lies, promises, stars, and mythical rivers. Instead, there is a collective "we" who swarms. The swarm shows up in the book's form, vividly reminding us that literature ain't the only way to literacy. With the Hades series, for instance, Samiya continues an ongoing collaboration with mixed-media artist Alison Saar. Originating with the sculptural work *Hades D.W.P.*, Samiya and Alison use glass jugs, etching, water, spoons, and cloth labels to depict survival—a story as old as Blackness and water. The only way through is to breathe. And while we see versions of their collaboration documented throughout the book, readers can also take each image as a prompt to seek out and encounter the physical sculpture. Sometimes you must leave the book to keep reading.

In her book *Field Theories*, Samiya "subjected poetry to physics," breaking theorems open and remaking bodies with celestial flair. In *I Hope This Helps*, she is a poet-cartographer, traversing multiple worlds. In one instance, a world is defined by a young Samiya, still a child, taking in all she could overhear from the grown folks around her. Another world is one of exile forged through the onslaught of a global pandemic. And yet another world, interior and private, is shaped by the author's encounters with her past. These worlds coexist. They are shaped by experiences, real and imagined. They are fueled by the alchemy of our will. They stretch beyond the Earth and into the stars, override historical fact, and tread the rivers of Hades. Samiya treats the cosmos and underworld as context, not metaphor, because this earthly realm is not the only place we exist. Haven't you ever lived with your head in the stars?

This is the experiment you've been waiting for.

DR. DERRAIS CARTER
Somewhere in Rhode Island
July 2024

NOTES ON MULTIMEDIA & COLLABORATIVE POETRIES

Explore *I Hope This Helps* Beyond the Page

Scan this QR code (how very 2020 of the book) to experience the unique fusion of poetry, video, visual art and music, that make up *I Hope This Helps*. Let this immersive experience deepen your connection with the words and sounds that shape this work.

The work in this book features poetries that cross genres, modes, and media, including copious collaborations with composers and visual artists, as detailed below. Although so much of this book was drafted during some of the most isolated months and years of my life – Such exile! So locked down!—none of this could I alone have written. I mean—we can get all woo-woo about it (no, really, we can), but also there are the practicalities of collaborative art-making as the practice I love so passionately.

I've got to begin at the end because this book gave me the untraditional opportunity to work collaboratively with designer Kit Schluter, who helped me bring to life the transliteration of this poetry into book form. The weeks and days and hours upon hours of care taken to reshape these multimedia poetries, including the creation of an original linocut print for the cover image, are all indicative of Kit's generosity and care throughout this process.

The book is organized around a collaborative project built over time and across multiple media. In its original form, I collaborated with Alison Saar on the 2016 sculptural piece, "Hades D.W.P."—etched glass jars, water, dye, wood, cloth, and ink transfer, electronics, found ladles and cups, 30 x 50 x 16 in. (76.2 x 127 x 40.6 cm)—which was first exhibited as part of Saar's 2016 exhibition *Silt, Soot and Smut* (L.A. Louver, 2016).

"Hades D.W.P. [Department of Water and Power]" is, as noted in Denise Stewart-Sanabria's 2017 review of the work in a subsequent exhibition, *Breach,* "an indictment of the failure of Flint, Mich., to provide safe drinking water to its citizens, filtered through Greek mythology. Five jars of alarmingly colored 'drinking' water sit on a shelf, each with an accompanying drinking ladle. Each jar is named after one of the five rivers of death: Acheron, the river of pain; Phlegethon, the river of fire; Lethe, the river of forgetfulness; Styx, the river of hatred; and Cocytus, the river of wailing. Bashir's sharp and minimal prose, delicately transferred onto sheer fabric, beats out insistent phrases that call for awareness." In 2018, Alison and I worked with letterpress artist Tracy Schlapp to create the limited-edition 2018 Artists' Book, *Hades D.W.P.,* from which each linocut image, alongside its paired poem, is reproduced here to open a section of this book.

I worked again with Tracy Schlapp and visual artist Yornel J. Martínez Elías on the limited-edition Artists' Book, "M A P S :: a cartography in progress," exhibited as a part of 2016's *Intersecciones: Havana/Portland,* at the Hoffman Gallery of Contemporary Art. Some of that imagery can be found as a part of this book's virtual experience.

Collaboration here also exists at the formal level. "M A P S :: a cartography in progress" is an incomplete, and incompletable, found poem. I offer my deepest gratitude to epochal Somali novelist Nuruddin Farah for his work, especially the "Blood in the Sun" series, in whose third novel, *MAPS,* all of the language in "M A P S :: a cartography in progress" was pulled through an erasure of sorts, an autumn raking of leaves as tailored bibliomantic practice.

I am also deeply indebted to my musical and video collaborators as well. I worked with video artist Roland Dahwen Wu to produce the video component for "M A P S :: a cartography in progress." While the video has been shown in multiple exhibitions, including "I Hope This Helps," it also lives in performance along with my body, and various (often edible) interactive ephemera.

I wrote poems and libretti for two pieces with Joel Thompson (*Clairvoyance* and *Dark Matters*). For "Dark Matters" (available on your favorite streaming app as well as through this book's virtual experience), Joel and I worked through the depths of the pandemic to create a devastatingly personal choral piece, commissioned by Lynda Hasseler for the Capital University Chapel Choir.

For "Clairvoyance," I worked with Joel Thompson to create a videopoetic choral piece for the 2021 festival, Prototype—Opera | Theatre | Now, featuring Rhianna Cockrell, Deborah Johnson, and Andrea Walker. I rented a car and drove from Pandemic Exile to New Haven, Connecticut, to direct the video for "Clairvoyance" alongside video artist Camilla Tassi, with whom I also worked on the video for "Here's the Thing:".

The poem, "Here's the Thing:", arrived during the process of writing the libretto of the same name with composer Julian Wachner. "Here's the Thing:" was commissioned by The Washington Chorus in 2019 and completed in 2020. It was originally commissioned and created for full orchestra and chorus to open the Washington Chorus' first new season with Artistic Director Eugene Rogers (a Negro First(TM) for the Chorus), which lost its Kennedy Center opening due to the pandemic. Linked to this virtual experience is a virtual video excerpt of the piece for piano, created for Zoom during lockdown and presented in 2021. The full piece has yet, as of this printing, to be performed.

"who's osmosin' who" was commissioned and written as a part of *Black Revelry,* a multimedia publication in honor of Ernie Barnes' iconic 1976 painting "The Sugar Shack" (acrylic on canvas, 36 x 48 in.) for which each author chose a specific piece of the painting to which their work responds. Check the poem, and the painting, to see which section I chose.

:: Finally, A Note on the Standards ::

These poster-like pages are re-visioned from an ongoing installation exhibition: **I Hope This Helps, 2020,** Ink and acrylic on cloth, wire, brackets, 20 pieces, 2m x 1.25m each. This work has so far been featured in three exhibitions: "Cinque Mostre: Convergence," the American Academy in Rome, 2020; "I Hope This Helps," The Africa Center NYC, 2024; and "I Hope This Helps," Michigan State University Poetry Center, 2025.

Standard:

- [heraldry] a long, tapering flag or ensign, as of a monarch or a nation
- a form of language widely accepted as the usual form
- a rule or principle used as a basis for judgment
- an upright support or supporting part
- a distinct petal, larger than the rest
- a vexillum

These 20 Standards each herald a moment of sight or of blindness, a call for help, an offer of assistance, an insistence. Built to take the place of the artist's body in performance, the poem's place within the pages of a book, and the conversations we too often relegate to therapy or theory, these Standards instead invite the experiencer's body to step into the work itself.

Sound and space guide experiencers down different avenues than expected as each Standard is met. "I Hope This Helps" represents the aural qualities of poetry and the sound of the artist's voice through the trickle of the neighboring fountains and the flap of each Standard in the wind. These interactions—body, nature, text, handprint, fabric, movement–work to light the world as it is built and the body as it responds to that built environment.

The Standards challenge experiencers to engage controversial issues and erosive emotions outside of more limiting "standard" frameworks. Consider, for example, a concept such as "racist" not as identity or character trait but as inescapable cultural inheritance that can be identified and unlearned. If the opposite of "racist" shifts from "not racist" to "antiracist" then the standard shifts from judgment to action. As we move through each Standard, they too move and shift, each an invitation and a welcome toward mutual understanding, movement, and change.

ACKNOWLEDGMENTS

I would also like to acknowledge my appreciation for the following publications in which some of this work has appeared, occasionally in different form:

- "Per Aspera," *Zyzzyva*, Issue No. 128, Fall 2024
- "Untie," *Orion Magazine*, Autumn 2024 (special broadside insert)
- "negro being :: freakish beauty," *A Mouth Holds Many Things,* Dao Strom and Jyothi Natarajan, editors, Fonograf Editions, 2024
- "Wabenzi Walks," *Invisible Strings*, Kristie Frederick Dougherty, ed., 2024
- "Phlegethon," "Acheron," "Cocytus," Lethe," "Styx," *Hades, D.W.P.* (limited edition Artists Book), with Alison Saar and Tracy Schlapp, 2019
- "M A P S :: a cartography in progress," *CLOCKHOUSE*, Volume Four, Folio editor Bhanu Khapil, 2016
- "Hurry up please, it's closing time," *Ki / Qui Parle*, 2023
- "Some days of wine and pastry"—*Poem-a-Day*, poets.org, September 2023
- *MAPS: a cartography in progress* (limited edition Artists Book), with Yornel J. Martínez Elías and Tracy Schlapp, Intersecciones: Havana/Portland, Ronna and Eric Hoffman Gallery of Contemporary Art, Lewis & Clark College, 2016
- "i traveled the world. it was fine."—*Poem-a-Day*, poets.org, July 2021
- "nail hard," *Poetry Magazine*, 2024

- "The Only Poem," "Greenwich means," "Where Mosquitoes Go During the Day," "Plane After Plane After Plane Buzzes," *Obsidian Journal,* GenderQueer/GenreQueer Playground, Ronaldo Wilson ed., 2023
- "Lethe," "Phlegethon," "Acheron," *Indiana Review 44.2*, Winter 2023
- "Here's the Thing:" *Freeman's Journal,* John Freeman, editor, Penguin 2022
- "who's osmosin' who," *Black Revelry,* D.A. Carter, ed. Amsterdam, NL, 2022
- "Letter from Exile," *There's a Revolution Outside, My Love,* eds. Tracy K. Smith & John Freeman, Vintage Books, 2021
- "negro being :: freakish beauty," *On Black Aliveness, Interim Magazine,* Ronaldo Wilson, editor, Volume 37, Issues 3–4, 2021
- "Another Thin Filament Pyrometry," "Sometimes in a body," *Heard Immunity*, MoMA/PS1, Gregg Bordowitz, editor, 2020
- "HOW NOT TO STAY UNSHOT IN THE U.S.A.," *Ecotone Magazine,* Various Instructions, 2020
- "You're really faithful to your abusers, aren't you?" *Poem-a-Day,* Academy of American Poets, Dawn Lundy Martin, editor, 2018

Thank you to The American Academy in Rome, The Africa Center (NYC), and Michigan State University's Poetry Center, each of whom has shown the installation exhibition of "I Hope This Helps," and all of those who have supported this work with exhibitions, commissions, residencies, fellowships, grants, and more, without which *I Hope This Helps* could not have found its voice:

- "negro being :: freakish beauty," *A Mouth Holds Many Things,* a De-Canon group exhibition, Stelo Arts, 2024
- "Hades D.W.P.," with Alison Saar (2016, etched glass jars, water, dye, wood, cloth and ink transfer, electronics, found ladles and cups, 30 x 50 x 16 in.), 2016 (multiple showings)
- "I Hope This Helps," solo exhibition, The Africa Center, May-August 2024

- "Dark Matters," librettist: Samiya Bashir; composer: Joel Thompson; Capital College Conservatory of Music, Dr. Lynda Hasseler Director, World Premier, 2023
- "Here's the Thing:," poet: Samiya Bashir, composer: Julian Wachner, Kennedy Center, Washington DC, libretto commissioned by the Washington Chorus *performance postponed indefinitely due to COVID.* Virtual piano excerpt, 2021, "Here's the Thing:," performed excerpt for REVELRY, The Washington Chorus, virtual premiere.
- "Clairvoyance," libretto for collaborative choral video short, composer: Joel Thompson, video artist: Camilla Tassi, *Prototype Festival: opera | theater | now,* 2021

Thank you to New York City for welcoming me back home in the storm. Thank you to the Pacific Northwest for letting me go so lovingly. Thank you to the following organizations which have supported my work and process over the making of this book: allgo, The Africa Center, the American Academy in Rome, Atlantic Center for the Arts, De-Canon, Fine Arts Work Center, MacDowell, New York State Council on the Arts, Saints + Sinners LBGBT Literary Festival, Sculpture Space, Truro Center for the Arts at Castle Hill, Regional Arts and Culture Council, and the Virginia Center for Creative Arts.

GRAZIE, RAGAZZI

With various and willy-nilly body parts, including, especially, my heart, I humbly thank the extraordinary people who have walked with me through this journey, laying down tracks when I couldn't, sliding pennies and dimes onto the tracks when I needed a smash, holding me up when I felt like I might fall across those tracks, bringing their magic into my world. To my family—all of you—especially my parents, my sisters and brothers, my power-cousins (D9!), and my coven of aunties—Gloria Banks, Amy Hilliard, and Wendy Hilliard—you are my foundation, my heart, my home, and I am forever grateful for your love. There are innumerably more people than I can name here, but what I must do is name as many of those without whom the realization of this work would not have been possible as I can. So many of you know exactly what you've done, how you've kept me upright. Some of you likely have no idea—of the ways in which, by your very being and doing, you save(d) me..

Alphabetically, because let's be real, how else?

I call to Nina Chanel Abney, Naa Akua, Philip Alexander, Kazim Ali, Jafari Allen, and J. Bob Alotta, thank you for your relentless encouragement and support. To Darwin Aquino, Byllye Avery, Dzidzor Azaglo, Stephen Beaudoin, John Beer, Alexandra Bell, Jen Bervin, Lindsey Boldt, Todd Boss, Garrett Bradley, and Sharon Bridgforth—your creativity has been a lighthouse guiding me through every storm. And Jericho Brown, Courtney Bryan, Richard Burns, Daniela Candillari, Dr. Derrais Carter, Monica Carter, James Casebere, and Victor Cazares—you have pushed me to dream bigger, to work harder, and to see the world through a lens I might have missed.

Jae Choi, Chrysanthemum, Cheryl Clarke, Lisa Coleman, Paris Cian Cyan, Jessie Daniels, Helga Davis—I wouldn't be here without you, your support, your friendship, your generosity, and your wisdom. Kirstie Darko, Michaela Angela Davis, Kelsey Day, Alexis DeVeaux, Dyani Douse, R. Erica Doyle, Camille Dungy, Elisa Durrette, and Torkwase Dyson—thank you for being the kind of people who show up, every time, in every way that matters.

I am endlessly grateful to Hassan Elahi, Chloe Feffer, Lorraine Ferguson, bart fitzgerald, Laura Flanders, Novella Ford, T'ai Freedom Ford, Aricka Foreman, for your fierce support and unwavering love. Jade Foster, Vievee Francis, Krista Franklin, John Freeman, Lisa Freeman, Steven G. Fullwood, Keyon Gaskin, Theaster Gates, Ephen Glenn, Farah Jasmine Griffin, and Ryan Gray—your brilliance lifts me higher, your art keeps me inspired. To Alexis Pauline Gumbs, Ashley Hahn, Minal Hajratwala, Duriel Harris, Reginald Harris, Saidiya Hartman, Lynda Hasseler, Terrance Hayes, Justine Henning, and Laurie Hollinger.

To the geniuses who are Erica Hunt, Uzodinma Iweala, Sara Jaffe, John Jesurun, Daniel Alexander Jones, Gia & Gina Jones, Kellie Jones, and Omi Oshun Joni Jones—your presence in my life is pure light. A. Van Jordan, Alexandra Juhasz, Naima Karsczmar, John Keene, Sameer ud Dowla Khan, and Ruth Ellen Kocher—you've held me down, and I am deeply thankful for your love and constant support.

Charlotte LaGarde, L.D. Lewis, Glenn Ligon, Arleta Little, Sharon Louden, Maggie Lower, Yvette Loynaz, Ngina Lythcott—you have been there at my most critical junctures, and I carry your energy with me. Rajendra Ramoon Maharaj, my Hooyo: Halima Mao, Aurielle Marie, Nicole Mason, BJ Mensah, Bobby Mensah, KC Mensah, Adrian Matejka, Terry McGovern, Tony Medina, Julie Mehretu, Dante Micheaux, Shawn Miller, June Mines, Cherie Mittenthal, Lisa C. Moore, Fred Moten, Stephen Motika, Jade Novarino, Narumi Tei Okamoto, and Okwui Okpokwasili—you are all creative powerhouses, and I am forever inspired by the magic you make.

Matthew Olzmann, John Oschendorf, Evelyn Owen, Gala Prudent, Tanya Puig, Claudia Rankine, Cathy Renna, Anastasia Renée, Favour Ritaro, Rashad Robinson, Peter Rock, Eugene Rogers—thank you for seeing me, and for your continued friendship and grounding presence. Alison Saar, Pancho Savery, Tracey Schlapp, Sarah Schulman, A.O. Scott, Nicole Sealey, Diane Seuss, Ziaire Sherman, Sonya Shields, Leslie Shipman, David Simpson, Christopher Stahling, Lisa Steinman, Gabriel Stover, K.M.A. Sullivan, Dan Sullivan, LaShandra Sullivan, Tawanna Sullivan—you've shown up in ways that make me believe in the beauty of community.

Camilla Tassi, Del'Shawn Taylor, Michelle Tea, Joel Thompson, Azure B. Thompson, Jet Toomer, Adrienne Torf, Sharita Towne, Mai Tran, Naima Tukonow, Imani Uzuri, Santi Valencia, Linda Villarosa, Julian Wachner, Lilly Wachowski, Adam Weinberg, Marvin K. White, Antoine Williams, Phillip B. Williams, Kimberly Wilson, Mabel O. Wilson, Ronaldo V. Wilson, Jacqueline Woodson, Roland Dahwen Wu, Avery Young—your love has sustained me in ways I can't fully express. And finally, to Pamela Z, whose voice, a constant echo, remains such a powerful force in my life, and Erik Zornik, who has literally held my fading beloved life in his hands, and because how else would I know that transgender frogs are my jam and also that solidarity around equity can be real, real, real.

To my students, past and present—you've taught me as much as I've taught you. Likely more. To the so many doctors who've kept me alive, and to every lover of this past decade (and the one before, and the one to come)—you are a part of my heartbeat.

Each of you is the rhythm that keeps me moving forward. However I can stand, I stand and thank you.

© NINA JOHNSON

SAMIYA BASHIR, called a "dynamic, shape-shifting machine of perpetual motion" by Diego Báez, writing for *Booklist*, is a poet, writer, librettist, performer, and multi-media poetry maker whose work, both solo and collaborative, has been widely published, performed, installed, printed, screened, experienced, and Oxford comma'd from Berlin to Düsseldorf, Amsterdam to Accra, Florence to Rome, and across the United States. Sometimes she makes poems of dirt. Sometimes zeros and ones. Sometimes variously rendered text. Sometimes light. Bashir is the author of three poetry collections, most recently *Field Theories*, winner of the 2018 Oregon Book Award's Stafford/Hall Award for Poetry. Samiya's honors include the Rome Prize in Literature, the Pushcart Prize, Oregon's Arts & Culture Council Individual Artist Fellowship in Literature, plus numerous other awards, grants, fellowships, and residencies including MacDowell, the Atlantic Center for the Arts, and the New York Council on the Arts. In addition to her books, Bashir has served as editor to national magazines and anthologies of literature and artwork. Bashir currently serves as the June Jordan Visiting Scholar at Columbia University's Institute for Research in African American Studies. She lives / ~~on the road~~ / in Harlem.

NIGHTBOAT BOOKS

Nightboat Books, a nonprofit organization, seeks to develop audiences for writers whose work resists convention and transcends boundaries. We publish books rich with poignancy, intelligence, and risk. Please visit nightboat.org to learn about our titles and how you can support our future publications.

The following individuals have supported the publication of this book. We thank them for their generosity and commitment to the mission of Nightboat Books:

Kazim Ali • Anonymous (4) • Ava Aviva Avnisan • Jean C. Ballantyne • Will Blythe • V. Shannon Clyne • Theodore Cornwell • Ulla Dydo Charitable Fund • Gisela Gamper • Photios Giovanis • Amanda Greenberger • David Groff • Parag Rajendra Khandhar • Katy Lederer • Shari Leinwand • Elizabeth Madans • Ricardo Maldonado • Ethan Mitchell • Caren Motika • Elizabeth Motika • Asker Saeed • The Leslie Scalapino - O Books Fund • Amy Scholder • Thomas Shardlow • Benjamin Taylor • Jerrie Whitfield & Richard Motika • Clay Williams

This book is made possible, in part, by grants from the National Endowment for the Arts, New York City Department of Cultural Affairs in partnership with the City Council, and the New York State Council on the Arts Literature Program.

Large. fly

:: Fly conjure

Sleepless drop :: (secret)

large conjure dr

:) :: **Large**

Sit. Drop. Conjure. Fl

Large. *(secret)* Sit. Sleepless.

Conjure.

Sleepless. **Large.** *(secret)*

Large.

Sleepless drop (secret)

large conjure dr

Sit. :: Drop. Conjure. Fl

(secret) Sit. Sleepless.

Conjure. ::

Sleepless. **Large.** *(secret)*

Large.

Sleepless drop (secret)

large :: conjure dr

Sit. :: Drop. :: Conjure. :: F